GOD WORDS

GOD WORDS

An Introduction to Classic Christian Theology

CONCORDIA PUBLISHING HOUSE • SAINT LOUIS

2 3 4 5 6 7 8 9 10   13 12 11 10 09 08 07

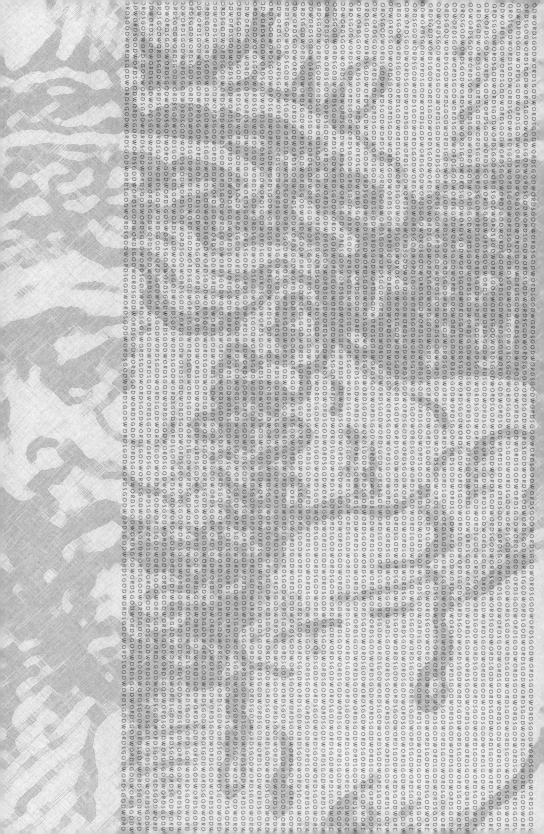

Table of Contents

Introduction

A highly respected theologian was asked, "Why do you like theology?" He said simply, "Because I love talking about God!" He could not have been more right. The word *theology* comes from two Greek words—*Theos*, which means "God," and *logos*, which means "word." Theology means simply, "God words." Whenever people talk or think about God, they are doing theology. Christianity is, first and foremost, about Jesus Christ. All that we do, and all that we are, has to do with Jesus Christ. His words are forever true: "I am the vine; you are the branches" and "Apart from Me you can do nothing" (John 15:5). Christian theology is the study and proclamation of the good news about Jesus Christ.

The Bible tell us not to be satisfied with spiritual baby food, but to hunger for good, wholesome, solid food. "Grow in the grace and knowledge ..." (2 Peter 3:18). In other words, God is telling us to grow up! We are to immerse ourselves in the Word of God, the Holy Bible, and to continue our studies and reflections on the person and the work of Jesus Christ and all that the Word of God teaches us.

What passes for "spirituality" these days leaves many people unsatisfied and malnourished. They realize they are on spiritual starvation diets. They search for a satisfying spiritual life and discover it in the treasures of classic Christian theology. As they do, they realize the joy of a life with God anchored in the concrete realities of our Lord's Word and Sacraments. As they search further, they find what they are looking for in the oldest continuing evangelical movement in the history of Christianity. They find what they are looking for in Lutheranism. Lutheranism does not throw out the good, noble, and beautiful treasures and traditions of classic Christianity. Instead it focuses them all through the lens of a powerful Gospel-centered theology.

So, enjoy this collection of "God words." Read each chapter carefully and thoroughly. Look up the Bible verses used in each chapter. Work your way through the discussion questions, either by yourself or, if you are able, with a group of fellow Christians. The peace of Christ be with you!

The Publisher

The Bible As God's Word

BY JOHN JOHNSON

The Message

Great emphasis is placed on communication in our world. Businesses specializing in computers and communications systems have been among the fastest growing in the market. Communications media (newspapers, television, radio, etc.) have great influence on public opinion and remain the prime source for our knowledge of current events. Politicians, preachers, and public figures are evaluated on their skills as "great communicators." The communications field is a popular major for college students.

God is concerned with communication too! He has made mankind in such a way that we are able to communicate with Him in prayer and praise. God has given us the gift of words to do this.

But more important, God Himself is a communicator. No one can tell us what God wants us to believe and to do but God Himself. This is the meaning of revelation—that in His grace and concern for people God makes Himself known. He becomes the "revealed" God for us. But how does this communication take place?

Of course, God spoke to mankind personally and directly in His own Son, Jesus. The author of the Book of Hebrews writes, "In the past God spoke to our forefathers through the prophets at many times and in various ways, but in these last days He has spoken to us by His Son, whom He appointed heir of all things, and through whom He made the universe" (Hebrews 1:1–2). In its most basic meaning, the Word of God is Jesus Christ. "In the beginning was the Word. . . . The Word became flesh and made His dwelling among us" (John 1:1, 14).

We have no knowledge of Christ apart from the Bible, the written communication of God. Watching a magnificent sunset or gazing at the majestic Rocky Mountains may indeed tell us something about our heavenly Father's creative power and the beauty of His creation, but it tells us nothing about Jesus. The wonders of nature tell us nothing about the will of God and His plan of salvation.

Christians believe that the Bible is the means God uses in communicating with us today. In the Holy Scriptures, God tells us of Christ and His death on the cross for the forgiveness of our sins. He tells us about His will for all mankind. He even tells us about His plan for our own lives. God can communicate only truth, and the Bible serves as the perfect source and guide for our knowledge of Him.

But the Bible does not work like a magical formula. As in any communication between persons, God's Word must be read, studied, meditated upon, digested, and reviewed to be understood. To further understanding, it helps to know the general character and purpose of the Bible as God's Word.

The Inspiration of the Bible

Belief in the Bible as God's Word is frequently questioned. Many religious groups, some of them very popular, have a "sacred book" that claims to be of divine origin. Muslims rely on the Qur'an. Mormons have Joseph Smith's Book of Mormon. Other groups place their trust in the sayings of individual prophets and teachers who set forth "messages from God." How can Christians say that our Bible is really the Word of God?

Inspiration is a key word in attempting to answer this question. We speak of Scripture as the inspired Word of God because the men who wrote it were moved by the Holy Spirit to write what God Himself wanted to communicate.

The word *inspired* is a familiar one. We sometimes use it to describe a great artist, poet, or musician. We say that Shakespeare was "inspired" to write great plays or that Beethoven was "inspired" to produce great symphonies. We may even use the word to speak of ourselves occasionally—"I was so inspired by Coach's pep talk in the locker room that I put extra effort into that last touchdown run" or "I was inspired to become a teacher because of my English teacher, Mrs. Smith."

The biblical meaning of "inspiration" is uniquely different. The word actually means "God-breathed." It refers not to the human talents and abilities of the writers, but to what is written. There is only one "God-breathed" book—the Bible.

Can we prove that the Bible is truly the inspired Word of God? Should proving it even be our desire when sharing our faith with friends? The answer to both questions: "No, not really."

That may sound like a startling statement, but think a moment about how we usually prove a fact. In science class you prove the cell structure of blood by smearing a drop on a slide and placing it under a microscope. But blood is a natural substance, subject to scientific examination.

When we talk about divine inspiration, we speak of a miraculous process, a supernatural process. The divine origin of Scripture is actually a conviction worked in our heart by the Holy Spirit. In a sense, the Bible provides its own best "argument." Our continued study of Scripture will do more than any human logic or scientific analysis to strengthen our confidence in its divine origin and character.

This does not mean that certain external considerations are totally unimportant. Exciting archaeological discoveries that confirm biblical stories, personal testimonies of changed lives that come from reading the Bible, the survival of the Scriptures through long centuries of criticism and assault—these facts all attest to the inspiration of Scripture. But we cannot judge the Bible from the outside. We must get inside, and then we will know with assurance that it is God's communication with us.

The Bible itself claims to be the inspired Word of God. The apostle Paul writes in 2 Timothy 3:16, "All Scripture is God-breathed and is useful for teaching, rebuking, correcting and training in righteousness." 2 Peter 1:20–21 is another important statement: "No prophecy of Scripture came about by the prophet's own interpretation. For prophecy never had its origin in the will of man, but men spoke from God as they were carried along by the Holy Spirit." Both of these passages emphasize the divine origin of the Bible. They also reveal two specific points helpful for our understanding of inspiration.

First, there is nothing in our Bible that was not inspired. All of Scripture was produced by the life-giving breath of God. This truth can often be difficult for us to understand. Be honest! How many times have you decided to read sections of the Bible each night before going to sleep, and then found yourself nodding because the passages you were reading seemed to be irrelevant? You simply could not take any more accounts of kingdoms and battles, family trees and love stories! So many passages of Scripture seem to deal with trivial matters. You are absolutely right. Don't feel guilty for thinking it!

There is a difference in respect to the importance of the various things recorded in the Bible. But remember—something may be of minor importance according to human wisdom, but very important when viewed against the whole purpose of God. He had a reason for communicating to us what He did.

Romans 15:4 says, "For everything that was written in the past was written to teach us, so that through endurance and the encouragement of the Scriptures we might have hope." Valuable lessons for everyday living frequently emerge from passages that at first glance appear relatively insignificant. In other words, there is no distinction in the Bible between passages written by divine inspiration and passages that are not. It is all inspired.

A second important point concerning the inspiration of the Bible is that God "moved" individual human beings to write it. Scripture does not communicate to us in a "spiritual" language that no one can understand. And this does not mean that the authors of the Bible were just writing machines. God did not punch them, like keys on a computer, to produce His message. You may recall seeing or reading about psychics who perform what is called "automatic writing." They supposedly receive messages from the "other side" by falling into a trance, taking pen to paper, and without knowing what they are doing, writing out what is dictated by their "spirit guide." This is not the way God inspired the writers of the Bible. He did not destroy the personalities of Moses, David, John, Paul, and others whom He inspired to write.

Each writer used his own personal style, arranged his thoughts, and constructed his sentences. Their writings bear the imprint of their times and reproduce the local color of the places where they were composed. Further, they knew what they were doing and writing. David, for example, knew that the Spirit of God spoke through him (2 Samuel 23:2). St. Paul was fully conscious when he wrote his epistles (2 Thessalonians 3:17). Yet God worked through these human personalities. He guided and controlled men and His Spirit so that what they wrote is what He wanted written.

Other claims of the supernatural origin of the Scriptures are sprinkled throughout the Bible. The Old Testament prophets spoke as "mouthpieces" of God (Jeremiah 1:9). Later writers of Scripture quote passages written earlier as words spoken by God (Galatians 3:8). New Testament writers claim to have the same prophetic authority as Old Testament writers (Matthew 11:9–15; 1 Corinthians 14:37).

Most important of all, however, is how Jesus Himself viewed Scripture. What did our Lord think of it? How did He use it? Jesus quoted Scripture as His final authority, often introducing the statement with the phrase "It is written," as in His encounter with Satan in the wilderness (Matthew 4). He spoke of Himself and of events surrounding His life as being fulfillments of Scripture (Matthew 26:54–56). He declared that Scripture cannot be broken (John 10:35). Indeed, it was the Lord who promised His disciples the Holy Spirit, who will "teach you all things and will remind you of everything" (John 14:26), who will also "guide you into all truth" (John 16:13).

How strange it would be to reject Scripture as God's inspired Word, yet at the same time believe in Jesus Christ as our Savior. We would be in disagreement with the very One whom we confess to be the eternal Son of God!

The Properties of the Bible

Our conviction that the Bible is God's Word has important consequences. It is not just an abstract theory or a "dry-as-dust" dogma that has little effect on our Christian life. For example, since Scripture is the Word of God by divine inspiration, it also has certain traits—characteristics, features, properties—that help shape our study and use of it. The following traits are among the most outstanding.

Authority

We live in a world of conflicting authorities. Some statements are made on the authority of science, some on the authority of feeling and emotion, some on the authority of an institution or government. Much of our time in life is given over to sorting out the claims these various authorities have on us and placing them in proper order. What comfort we can take in knowing that God Himself stands behind every statement, promise, and command of the Bible.

How do you evaluate ideas and movements and teachings that demand a response? One philosophy comes along that says sex before marriage is perfectly acceptable. Another asserts that abortion is a right decision in every situation. One religious movement teaches that salvation depends on reaching a plane of God-consciousness. In the face of all of these, we look to God's Word. There is no greater authority! "If anyone teaches false doctrines and does not agree to the sound instruction of our Lord Jesus Christ and to godly teaching, he is conceited and understands nothing" (1 Timothy 6:3–4). Ultimate authority for the Christian is God's self-communication, centering in the Gospel of Christ, fully attested to and witnessed by the Word of Scripture.

Sufficiency

Why did God let Adam and Eve choose between good and evil when He must have known what they would do before they did it?

How did Noah get all of those animals on the ark?

Why do some people live and die without ever hearing the name of Jesus?

These questions and many others are often asked of Christians, and they become the source of frustration due to our inability to supply a quick answer. We become even more frustrated with the Bible for not giving those answers. But the problem lies not with the Bible, but with our expectations of it.

Scripture was not given to us in order to satisfy our curiosities about God's ways with humankind. It does not reveal all of the truth about God. It *does* reveal everything that we must know to be saved. It is sufficient for the accomplishment of its purpose—sufficient to "make [us] wise for salvation" and to educate us in righteousness of life (2 Timothy 3:15–16). God has communicated everything necessary for faith and life. While speculating on questions such as those noted above is often challenging, and for some people "fun," we must remind ourselves that for every such question there is not clear revelation. There exists knowledge about God which is in Him and which has never been revealed. But we can be confident that the Bible is sufficient to accomplish its end, namely, faith in Christ and eternal salvation.

Clarity

Have you ever come across a passage of Scripture that you simply could not understand? You pointed it out to your Sunday school teacher or your leader, and he or she could not give you a satisfactory explanation. You took it to your pastor, who admitted that even Bible scholars differ concerning the meaning of the verses. Then how can we say that a trait of Scripture is its "clarity"?

We do not mean that there are no difficult things in the Bible. Even the apostle Peter mentions that St. Paul's letters contain some statements that are hard to understand (2 Peter 3:16). Some difficult passages, perhaps the Book of Revelation comes immediately to mind, can be understood by using good principles of biblical interpretation (examination of the context, comparing less clear passages to plainer ones, recognizing the use of symbols, etc.). Others we may never absolutely understand due to our lack of knowledge regarding the situation to which they speak.

However, we can speak of the clarity of Scripture because what we need to know to be saved and to lead a God-pleasing life is clearly stated. It is clear, for example, that we cannot earn a good standing before God on the basis of the good works we perform. Because such teachings are clearly set forth in God's Word, it is a "light for my path" (Psalm 119:105). It can make the simple wise (Psalm 19:7).

Power

People view the Bible from many different angles. For some, it is just a book of rules to follow carefully if one wants to live a "good" life. For some, the Bible is a storybook filled with fascinating tales of heroes and villains. For others, it is a biography of a great religious teacher (*The Life and Times of Jesus of Nazareth*). There is an element of truth to all of these views, but for the Christian who acknowledges the Bible as God's Word, it is a powerhouse, a dynamo.

The Word of God operates in the hearts of those who hear and read it. It is imperative as Law and Gospel. The Word of Law is powerful. Like a hammer breaking rocks into pieces, the Law reveals our sinfulness and our rebellion against God. It shows our self-righteousness for what it really is. The Law is, as St. Paul says, no dead letter, but a letter that kills (2 Corinthians 3:6).

In contrast to the Law, the Word as Gospel gives life; it produces faith and hope (Romans 10:17). In its outward form the Gospel basically reports the life of Jesus. But it is more than a report, more than a biography. It relates the greatest needs of humankind.

Through the death and resurrection of Christ we are made alive. The Holy Spirit takes that Word and creates faith in the hearts of people.

John 6:63 says, "The words I have spoken to you are spirit and they are life." We have this assurance every time we seek guidance from the Word for our own lives or share its message with others. We wield power when we use the Word!

We have noted that God communicates to us through His written Word. On the face of it, the communication may seem haphazard. The Word contains 66 books with about 40 different authors, written over a period of more than 15 centuries. Each book has its own particular character and content. Yet it may be said that these writers point to one eternal truth.

This truth, like some jokes you hear, has bad news and good news. The bad news is about universal human sin: the truth that we "all have sinned and fall short of the glory of God" (Romans 3:23).

This bad news is answered by good news about a particular first-century Jew who is the Son of God and the Savior of the world. As God is its source, so Jesus Christ is the one central theme of Scripture. Both the Old and New Testaments bear witness to Him. The idea that we can choose between the two—take the Bible *or* Christ—simply does not work. Jesus is central to the plan of God, which the Bible reveals.

The church has taught much about the Bible as God's Word not mentioned in our discussion. Hopefully, some of the ideas and concepts brought to your attention in this essay will prompt further study and dialogue as you grow in your Christian faith.

One thing is sure: The Bible is as broad as life. It sets before us the history of redemption; the Law and the Gospel; God's promises, commands, works, and ways; lessons concerning faith and obedience. In short, God's communication involves every aspect of our existence. May He give us the grace to appreciate His message anew every day of our lives.

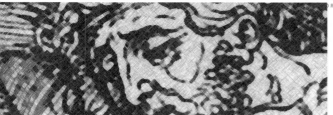

Discussion Questions

How does God reveal Himself?

How do we acquaint ourselves with His revelation?

What is "inspiration"?

How did God inspire His Word?

Who wrote the Bible?

If Scripture is inspired by God, why doesn't it all read exactly the same?

What authority does God's Word have for you?

How do you respond to that authority?

Why doesn't God answer every question in the Bible? What does He answer?

Does the Bible make mistakes? Why or why not?

If science and Scripture differ on a point, whose word will you take? Why?

What is the central theme of God's Word?

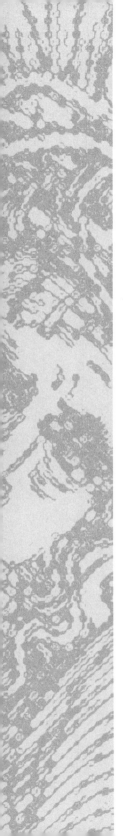

2

Creation

BY DEAN WENTHE

"In the beginning God created the heavens and the earth" (Genesis 1:1). God created everything in the universe including man and woman. Humankind was placed over God's creation as caretaker and steward. And for a while everything was perfect. Then sin entered the picture and things got messed up. Suddenly there were questions and doubts.

In some quiet moment a voice within may whisper, "What should I do with my life? Why am I here?" We can be sure that our answer will determine the course of our lives more than any other single decision or endeavor. It is not surprising that we often want to avoid such questions and decisions. Like gravity, the longing to know what we are and where we are going surrounds and holds each of us in its power.

These questions are not new. From the very beginning humanity has puzzled over what the world is and what role humankind plays in it. The great philosopher Aristotle urged that without this question humans ceased to be anything more than animals. "The unexamined life," he concluded, "is not worth living."

Ancient and modern men and women who have examined life have come to very different conclusions. The view that "all we are is dust in the wind" was popular among the intellectuals of early Greece, where one Epimenides had his tombstone inscribed with this statement: "Here lies Epimenides. I never married and I wish my father never had." To conclude one's life with such a statement says that person has examined life and found it completely without value.

All of us, at times, have felt the futility that so frustrated Epimenides. We seem to go in circles even when we acquire what we had looked forward to possessing. Somehow, there is always another something or someone that we think we need to possess.

Solomon, with all his wisdom, fame, and fortune, could still conclude that the whole world lacked an answer for the basic longing to know "For what?" "What does man gain from all his labor at which he toils under the sun? Generations come and generations go, but the earth remains forever" (Ecclesiastes 1:3–4).

Solomon rightly saw that the answer to who we are is tied to the question of what the world is. Do we appear for a moment like a spark above a campfire, only to disappear into the vast darkness of the world? Is humankind just an accidental occurrence as some scientists claim?

Christians have answered the questions "For what?" and "What is the world?" in a way that surprises and startles many people. It strikes the world so strangely that many don't even take the time to examine the answer. Young people may grow to maturity without a thorough talk about this peculiar option. It's easier to flip on the television or turn up the stereo than to discuss the subject of life's larger meaning.

The Christian's peculiar perspective, sometimes called faith, celebrates the goodness of life. It believes that humanity and its planet are part of a larger design. The Christian says that humankind is not a chance collision of atoms, but the peak toward which all else points, the pinnacle of all creation. Far from being caught in a world of meaninglessness, humans impart purpose to an otherwise decaying universe.

This perspective, Christians claim, comes quite naturally when the cross of Jesus Christ lifts mankind's vision beyond the exterior of molecules and matter to the interior of God's love.

Job, having lost far more than Epimenides, could still see that he was God's creature (Job 10):

"Your hands shaped me and made me" (verse 8).

"Remember that You molded me like clay" (verse 9).

"Did You not pour me out like milk and curdle me like cheese, clothe me with skin and flesh and knit me together with bones and sinews?" (verse 11).

"You gave me life" (verse 12).

Two very different answers! The epitaph of a tombstone testifies to despair and hopelessness. The conviction and confession of Job was that he was made by and for his great God.

At the cross, the question "For what?" finds a fulfilling and final answer. We are not here "for nothing." Rather, we are here for Someone—the great God who existed before all matter, brought all things into being, and still governs the galaxies. This great Creator of all things is also the God who is for us.

Man was made perfect, but he sinned and turned away from his Creator. When Adam walked away from God, the entire world was affected by his sin. As an old rabbi put it, "When God cried to Adam, 'Where are you?' it was not that God needed to know where Adam was, but that Adam now needed to know where God was."

Apart from God, all we find are the empty shells of dead or dying atoms. No matter how many times we split them, they tell us nothing about their ultimate origin. That's what humans continue to look for. What is our ultimate origin? Where did the earth and we come from? What is our purpose?

The cross has forever located God for Christians. In Jesus Christ, God demonstrated beyond all doubt that He and the world He created are for us. Christ took the most frustrating questions of "Who am I?" and "Where am I going?" and "What will I be when I grow up?" and wonderfully offered Himself as the answer.

In Christ we experience a love that supplies new life. In our Baptism we literally become a new creation. In His Word we find a new direction. In His Holy Supper we find food for our deepest hunger.

There is no nook or cranny of the universe that lacks the impact of Christ's incarnation. Our world and our being—body, soul, and spirit—are now new.

> *He is the image of the invisible God, the firstborn over all creation. For by Him all things were created: things in heaven and on earth, visible and invisible, whether thrones or powers or rulers or authorities; all things were created by Him and for Him. He is before all things, and in Him all things hold together. And He is the head of the body, the church; He is the beginning and the firstborn from among the dead, so that in everything He might have the supremacy. For God was pleased to have all His fullness dwell in Him, and through Him to reconcile to Himself all things, whether things on earth or things in heaven, by making peace through His blood, shed on the cross. (Colossians 1:15–20)*

The old, worn-out answers of this world now appear terribly dull and inadequate. Christians are living the truly fresh and creative life in a world that still packages the worn-out answers of the ancients.

This new reality, which the cross of Christ has opened for us, means that what we do with our lives will mirror Christ. We seem strange to those who are loaded down with old answers. Because of our new life we make the nitty-gritty daily decisions of life in a different way than those around us do.

When we hear "Am I worthless? Is my life meaningless?" from others or from within, Christ's love causes us to shout out, "No! Never! No way!" Not when the cross of Christ has demonstrated the infinite value of each person to the God who created and keeps all things forever.

Now and forever, I am a child of God. The angels delight when, led by the Spirit, one human reverses perspective, repents his/her old answers, and lifts open eyes to the ever new and fresh love that radiates from the cross.

Another question asked is, "Is my body evil?" Absolutely not! On the cross is a true human body that walked the dusty paths of a remote portion of our planet. Christ, the new life God sent for us, was not a ghost. He was and is for real! A good story. A grand sunset. The solitude of the wilderness. The beauty of a bird in flight. The matchless symmetry of the simplest flower. The marvelous melodies of music. Good food. Good friends. All of these things are to be enjoyed as we follow His life lived in space and time.

Can I enjoy my masculinity and femininity? Absolutely! The footsteps of new life turned toward a little village, where there was a big marriage celebration. He made new wine for the festivities! Christ affirmed and blessed the man-woman bond and urged fidelity as its divine mark (Matthew 19).

Far from missing out on the fun, the Christian knows the full meaning of sexuality. The larger love of the Christian couple for Christ makes their relationship ever new across the full spectrum of their beings—spiritually, emotionally, intellectually, and physically. Fidelity is seen as the freeing and fulfilling center of a lifelong bond between one man and one woman. Promiscuity and the exploitation of lustful desires are seen for what they are, a twisting abuse of something God created good.

Does the Christian view of the world and its origin contradict science? Here the answer hinges on the type of science and the type of Christianity that are in view. Some portrayals of science and some portraits of Christianity are based on the premise that there can be no peace between these two windows on the world.

The biblical story, however, holds that the God who created the heavens and the earth and the God who penetrated our planet in Christ are one. "Hear, O Israel: The LORD our God, the LORD is one" (Deuteronomy 6:4). Christians know that there is no ultimate contradiction between God's world and God's Word. The God who created and sustains and the God who acted in Israel and in Christ are one. Christians also acknowledge that God's Word (Holy Scripture) is focused on the loving disposition of a God who reaches out in Christ to rescue humankind from its distorted ways.

How long were the days of creation? When were the angels created? Where did Satan come from?

God has not thrown a set of encyclopedias to a drowning humanity! He sent His Son as described in the apostolic and prophetic Scriptures. As a result, God's Word does not address many of the questions that so quickly come to our modern (scientific) mind. Nor should such speculative concerns convert our confidence in Christ to that old cancer of forever asking, "For what?"

We are free in Christ to face the unfathomable mysteries of the universe. That Word, which was present at creation, came to re-create: "The blind receive sight, the lame walk, those who have leprosy are cured, the deaf hear, the dead are raised" (Matthew 11:5). Christ could do more than manipulate molecules. He, by His death and resurrection, withdrew the curse that encloses this old order. Thus, science, which senses the finiteness of its instruments, can simultaneously strive to explore the infinite nature of a fallen world.

Since science has helped humankind in concrete ways, it is not surprising that some have offered it as civilization's savior. Yet, such an offer is increasingly refused, for the knowledge that can help has also hindered humankind with the reality of nuclear holocausts.

The Christian is not surprised that no savior can come from scientific knowledge. The Garden of Eden forever established that without God, knowledge turns from blessing to curse. In the Garden of Gethsemane, on Golgotha, the curse was reversed. Christ has become our wisdom. We are blessed with a new perspective. We acknowledge the finiteness of our knowledge.

God's questions to Job (Job 38) are seen as more appropriate than any questions we might have for God.

"Who shut up the sea behind doors when it burst forth from the womb?" (verse 8).

"When I made the clouds its garment and wrapped it in thick darkness?" (verse 9).

"What is the way to the abode of light? And where does darkness reside?" (verse 19).

"Can you take them to their places? Do you know the paths to their dwellings?" (verse 20).

Our awareness that it is God who orders the world, and that God has appeared to us most fully in Christ, frees us from false perspectives.

No horoscope, no star chart, no Ouija board, no mathematical formula, no chemical equation, no unchangeable law, no biological evolution—none of these are in charge of the world's course. Rather, the God who has lovingly rescued us from the dead ends of sin and despair is also the God who governs all history and science and "provides me with all that I need to support this body and life" (Explanation of the First Article of the Apostles' Creed).

Divine providence works through such institutions as the family and the state to structure and define our lives. Even those who seek to exclude God from their world must move within the limits He has set.

Indeed, when Gentiles, who do not have the law, do by nature things required by the law, they are a law for themselves, even though they do not have the

law, since they show that the requirements of the
law are written on their hearts, their consciences
also bearing witness, and their thoughts now accus-
ing, now even defending them. (Romans 2:14–15)

This kind of universal awareness of what we "ought" or "ought not" do still marks humanity. Even though our intellect and will have been handicapped by the contagious consequences of the fall into sin, a fallen race still cannot escape the face of God's presence.

For what? We Christians propose the most profound answer that could be imagined. In fact, St. Paul says that such an answer could not have entered the heart of man (Galatians 1). We present the great triune God of Scripture—God the Father who created, God the Son who saved, and God the Holy Spirit who brings the answer of the Gospel to human hearts. The great reversal before the cross teaches us "For what?" We live a new life for God. The cross of Christ has forever established that this God is for us.

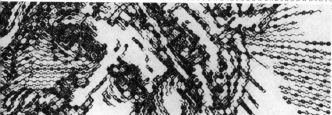

Discussion Questions

Why do we say that humankind is the high point of all creation?

For what was man created?

What is the significance of the cross of Christ in the matter of creation?

How can science and the Christian faith work together? Need they be at odds?

What is life for? What does that mean for your life?

3

The Doctrine of Man

BY JOHN JOHNSON

Who Am I?

Every human being has asked this question in his/her own way and in his/her own heart at one time or another. The quest for self-identity has been a human passion from the very beginning of history. There are, of course, different possible answers to the question. In a sense, who you are depends on whom you ask.

A scientist might respond, "You belong to the species of Homo sapiens. The cells in your body are developed out of the same substance as the cells of all animals on earth. Except for the cells in your brain, all others are renewed every seven years. Genetic research indicates that you are a single combination of factors out of 500 million possibilities. In the final analysis, you are an animal living on a second-rate planet attached to a second-rate sun."

A lawyer might say, "From the moment of your birth you are a citizen with certain rights and responsibilities. Your birth is immediately registered at a government office to insure your standing before the law. Once you reach the age of majority you may own property and sign contracts. You can vote and run for office. You can engage in business transactions. You can be prosecuted for criminal behavior."

At a wider level, an optimist might suggest, "Be proud! You are a part of humankind. Sure, we have our troubles and problems, but they are based on misunderstanding or lack of knowledge. If we just apply ourselves and try to be good to one another, things will surely get better."

On the other hand, the pessimist counters, "Man is basically evil. Look at his record! Wars, violence, cruelty, oppression, hatred, injustice. Man is rotten to the core. The future is only chaos. We are doomed."

All of these answers to the question "Who am I?" contain an element of truth. However, they are incomplete. Every humanly devised answer fails to account for all of the facts of our life and existence. If we are really to know ourselves—figure out *why* we do *what* we do, understand our relationships to others, recognize what it means to be a person—we must discover our identity in the very One who made us. "What is man that You are mindful of him?" (Psalm 8:4). God tells us who we are.

Man As Image of God

The first pages of the Bible tell about the origin of the world and man. They make clear that the world began in the mind of God and that He had a purpose for it. To be sure, God didn't need an earth or any other living thing to fulfill Himself. He didn't have to make mankind a part of His creation nor give us such a distinctive place in it.

> *Then God said, "Let Us make man in Our image, in Our likeness, and let them rule over the fish of the sea and the birds of the air, over the livestock, over all the earth, and over all the creatures that move along the ground." So God created man in His own image, in the image of God He created him; male and female He created them. God blessed them and said to them, "Be fruitful and increase in number; fill the earth and subdue it. Rule over the fish of the sea and the birds of the air and over every living creature that moves on the ground." (Genesis 1:26–28)*

God's Word says that we—all of us, male and female—were created in the image and likeness of God. Printed on a sheet of paper, that sentence can look pretty dead and uninspiring. But actually, this is such a radical thought that its meaning and implications are difficult for us to even grasp.

What does it mean to be "in the image of God"? Some thinkers have said that there is in this idea the suggestion of a physical likeness. They will point out that in various ancient myths man is made in the physical likeness of the deity. But clearly this cannot be the answer. God is not a material, physical being. "God is spirit" (John 4:24). Other interpretations have been offered: to be in the image of God means there is a mysterious "divine spark" in man's nature; it simply means we are co-workers with God in improving the world; it means we have the potential to achieve a state of perfection.

Yet when you think about it, the concept of man as the image of God should not be that hard to understand. Just before leaving the house for that big date, you probably stop in front of the hall mirror. What you see is a reflection of yourself. There is an image of your person in the mirror.

Now, man is not a reflection of how God looks. But he is a reflection of what God is. Out of all the things that God made, one of them was to be a reproduction and display of God Himself.

What is God? He is righteous and holy. Similarly, man at his creation was a perfect being. His intellect was perfect, and his will in every way agreed with the holy will of God.

Obviously, man was not on the same plane with God. He was not the Lord's equal. The reproduction, after all, is never as great or as powerful as the model. The Creator is superior to His creature. Even so, within the limitations of his given faculties, original man was as perfect and righteous as the God who "breathed into his nostrils the breath of life" (Genesis 2:7).

Moreover, man was healthy and pure. While any speculation about the physical characteristics of Adam and Eve is guesswork on our part (Martin Luther believed that Adam's "powers of vision exceeded those of the lynx" and his strength enabled him to manage "lions and bears"), there is no doubt that their environment was perfect and their time was spent in close fellowship with God. Had man stayed as he was, he would never have died. He was created to live forever. Like all that God made, man was "good" (Genesis 1:31).

From this biblical portrait of man as the "image of God" a variety of lessons can be drawn and applied to our lives as Christians.

The first lesson is that we, and all people, are persons of value. Scripture reveals that man was a special creation of God. After the fall into sin, man *remains* the creation of God. "God has made me," Luther writes in his explanation of the First Article of the Apostles' Creed. Although we continually frustrate His purposes, we always remain a being God cares for, protects, and blesses.

As broadly conceived, the "image of God" in man pertains to those essential marks of personhood. What, in other words, makes you a person? What distinguishes you from an animal? Man is different from animals in that he is rational, creative, and in a certain sense, free. Adam was able to distinguish and to name the creatures God brought to him (Genesis 2:19–20). The forbidden fruit was pleasant to the eyes of Eve, and she desired it (Genesis 3:6). The fact that God prohibited man from eating of the tree of knowledge (Genesis 2:16–17) shows that man is a *moral* creature. None of these things are marks of a mere animal. Indeed, it is man who is described in the Bible as being only "a little lower than the heavenly beings" and crowned "with glory and honor" (Psalm 8:5).

It is therefore proper to speak of the value of man. It is proper to rejoice in the great achievements of the human race, to marvel at the accomplishments of mankind in medicine, technology, art, music. We cannot help but stand in awe before what is done in the world, in the created order. How important this is especially for young Christians. We *should* enjoy life. We *should* participate in all of those beautiful experiences that are a part of our civilization and culture. There is genuine goodness in the world, and we need not always stop to ask if it is being done by a Christian before we can appreciate it!

A second important implication of being in the "image of God" is that He made man for a very definite purpose. "Let them rule over the fish of the sea and the birds of the air, over the livestock, over all the earth, and over all the creatures that move along the ground" (Genesis 1:26). God created man and gave him the whole earth. He was designated by God as the caretaker over creation.

We remain caretakers, or stewards, of God's creation today. Much emphasis has been placed on ecology and the need to care for natural resources. The Christian will see this as an important part of his responsibility. It is easy for us to take the "dominion" and literally run away with it—to take it as an excuse for the selfish use of God's creation and the manipulation of limited resources for our own purposes. Remembering that human beings, in contrast with every other created thing, become God's representatives will cause us to treat God's created world with respect.

Who Am I?

The biblical message is clear: you are the special creation of a loving God, the object of His love and sustenance. You are created in His image. You are the crown of creation, and you have dominion over it. You are you. But this does not exhaust what the Bible teaches about mankind. There is another word too.

Man As Sinner

What a wonderful world it might have been if human beings had only kept the "image of God." But they lost it. The Bible tells us that Satan tempted man to wonder whether God was giving him enough. He tempted man to disobey God. Man began to doubt God. He began to want more than God had given him. As a consequence, he fell into sin (Genesis 3:2–6).

Where did the "sinner" part of your identity begin? It did not begin last week at school when you spoke an unkind word about a classmate. It did not begin this morning when you found yourself too rushed for a brief time of prayer and Bible study. Your identity as "sinner" did not begin when you first made the decision to cheat on a difficult biology exam.

"Therefore, just as sin entered the world through one man, and death through sin, and in this way death came to all men, because all sinned" (Romans 5:12). The Lutheran church uses the phrase "original sin" to describe this situation. It means that the "sinner" part of our identity is in every person from the day of birth. Original sin is the opposite of original goodness. Our sins separate us from God and from one another.

Of course, sin takes many different forms. We use a lot of words to describe it: wrongdoing, falling short, disobedience. But in terms of the question "Who am I?" two aspects of sin are the most descriptive. These elements virtually jump out at us where the fall of man is recorded, and they find confirmation throughout Scripture.

The first element is that sin is rebellion against God. Do you remember the words of the tempter? Eat of the tree and "you will be like God" (Genesis 3:5). The centrality of God is replaced by the centrality of self. We replace God's will with our own. Because of our sinfulness, every human being seeks to occupy the center of his own little world.

A second aspect of sin is pride. We know from our own experience that pride takes many forms.

Pride in Power

The desire for power motivates many people. On the individual level, it is the desire to possess other people, to tyrannize them and own them. How often we are tempted to use other people for our own ends. We begin to see persons as tools rather than as fellow human beings created in God's image. On a broader level, a culture or a nation may displace God and demand total allegiance.

Pride in Knowledge

Knowledge is a part of our sinful nature also. From the time you began school, you were probably told that knowledge is the key to the future. If we possess enough knowledge we will be able to control our environment. Certainly, knowledge is important. Reason and intellect are gifts of God to His creature. But it is possible to take such pride in knowledge and place so much stress on it that reason becomes a final and ultimate judge of truth. Pride in knowledge leads to extreme skepticism regarding all spiritual values. The Book of Proverbs reminds us that "the fear of the LORD is the beginning of wisdom, and knowledge of the Holy One is understanding" (Proverbs 9:10).

Pride in Virtue

Perhaps the most dangerous of all forms of pride is pride in one's own virtue, or self-righteousness. It assumes that one's own estimate of good deeds, good life, and good reputation is identical with God's. "Well, I'm a pretty good person when all is said and done. I haven't killed anyone; I usually go to church; I tell the truth; I work hard and make good grades; I don't harm animals!" And on it goes. We think that because we are convinced of our goodness, God must share the same conviction.

All of these elements are part of that little word we use so often—*sin*. Sin is an arrogant desire for independence from God and His Law.

Where does it all lead? The key word in the scriptural analysis is death. Sin leads to death. In Christian teaching, death means separation. Spiritual death means to be separated or alienated from God in this life (Ephesians 2:1, 5). Physical death is separation of body and soul. Eternal death is everlasting separation from God.

Who Am I?

We return to that fundamental human question—now in the light of God's answer. The Bible does not define man from just one perspective or angle as the scientist or the lawyer or the psychologist would do. The Bible sees us as *persons*. We are creatures of God and reflect His image. We are persons of value. God is good, and He creates us good.

At the same time, the Bible teaches that man distorted and defaced the image. We are not *necessarily* sinful, but we are *in fact* sinful—inevitably and universally. Our love for others is often an act to disguise other motives, and we use the world for our own selfish purposes.

But this is not God's last word to us. According to our Creator's plan, Jesus Christ is Himself in the image of God. St. Paul writes, "For He has rescued us from the dominion of darkness and brought us into the kingdom of the Son He loves, in whom we have redemption, the forgiveness of sins. He is the image of the invisible God, the firstborn over all creation. . . . All things were created by Him and for Him. He is before all things, and in Him all things hold together" (Colossians 1:13–17).

In Christ, we know who we are. We are God's special, forgiven, loved people!

Discussion Questions

Based on your reading, what do you understand the "image of God" to be?

Why does man have value?

What does this chapter say to you about your sense of "self-worth" or "self-esteem"?

What is sin? Where did it come from?

What is the result of sin?

How is sin corrected?

How is man different from the rest of God's creatures?

How would you answer the question "Who am I?" for yourself?

4

Justification by Grace through Faith

BY DAVID LUMPP

GODWORDSGODWORDSGODWORDSGODWORDSGODWORDSGODWORDSGODWORDSGODWORDSGODWORD
WORDSGODWORDSGODWORDSGODWORDSGODWORDSGODWORDSGODWORDSGODWORDSGODWORDSGO
GODWORDSGODWORDSGODWORDSGODWORDSGODWORDSGODWORDSGODWORDSGODWORDSGODWORD

Rescued

In a very important sense the theme of the entire Bible is rescue. Perhaps a little more clearly, the theme of the Bible is God's rescue of sinful humanity.

Holy Scripture frequently emphasizes that we are all sinful. In fact, we are described rather bluntly by the apostle Paul as being "ungodly" (Romans 5:6). The sin that plagues us is not just a series of errors or wrong, possibly evil, things that a person does. Our sinful condition afflicts all humanity without exception. And, apart from Christ, such sin destroyed the relationship of man with God, so much so that it causes hostility between ourselves and God (Ephesians 2:16). There is no neutrality when it comes to our relationship with Him (Romans 8:6–8).

Sin actually kills you spiritually, and you cannot restore yourself to spiritual life or health. This is precisely what Paul means when he states that we are "dead in transgressions" (Ephesians 2:5). Put quite simply, spiritual rebirth is necessary. Nothing less will do. No resolution to improve oneself—however conscientious, well-intended, and diligent it might be—can get the job done. The damage is too severe. Help has to come from the outside.

The Bible tells us how God takes our plight into His hands. Scripture uses a variety of words and concepts to get this point across. One principal concept is "justification." To say that a person has been justified is to say that his or her sins have been forgiven. Justification means the forgiveness of sins; the two are synonymous.

Sin makes God angry; it cannot go unpunished. Why then does God forgive us? The biblical answer is grace. The concept of grace is so fundamental in Scripture (both in the Old and New Testaments) that we can say without exaggeration that salvation by grace is *the* distinctive truth of the Christian faith. The whole point is that our justification, our forgiveness, our salvation—our rescue—is due entirely to the grace of God.

First we must recognize that grace is underserved. God does not see anything *in us* that would prompt Him to forgive us. Mankind is hostile toward God and wants nothing to do with Him. So God takes the initiative. Thus grace is the undeserved mercy of God by which He forgives us and restores us to Himself. "For all have sinned and fall short of the glory of God, and are justified freely by His grace through the redemption that came by Christ Jesus" (Romans 3:23–24). It bears repeating, therefore, that grace is not in any way based on something that we can do or earn or accomplish. If that were the case, it would not be grace. It would be a reward.

Why Is God Gracious?

This question takes us back to the character of God. He is gracious because it is His nature to be gracious. We can say no more—and no less—than that!

Grace tells us why God forgives sin; it does not imply that He overlooks sin. As we said only a moment ago, sin must be punished. The Bible tells us in no uncertain terms that God does so. This introduces the most striking dimension of the scriptural account of our rescue from sin. Our Deliverer would give up His life in the process.

This realization enables us to complete the definition of grace begun above: God's grace is His undeserved mercy or love for the sake of His Son, Jesus Christ. Such an affirmation is absolutely central. There is no mercy or grace of God apart from Jesus Christ. In this sense, the life of the sinless Son of God is the "price" exacted by our sin.

This truth has both a Law and Gospel dimension. On the one hand, we see the frightening consequences of our sin (Law). Sin results in the wrath and judgment of God, and this in turn leads to nothing short of the death of the sinner. On the other hand, the crucifixion of Jesus in our place highlights the depth of the love of God and the lengths to which He was willing to go in order that we might be restored as His sons and daughters once again (Gospel). We have separated ourselves from God by our sin, but so intense is the Father's love for us that He actually casts Jesus from His presence rather than lose us for all eternity.

In a very real sense an exchange has taken place here, an exchange Luther called "blessed" or "fortunate." In this exchange God heaps our sins, all of them, onto the shoulders of Jesus. At the same time the Father takes Christ's perfect righteousness and confers it upon us. The depth of this exchange is vividly stated by St. Paul when he declares, "God made Him who had no sin to be sin for us, so that in Him we might become the righteousness of God" (2 Corinthians 5:21).

Another Look

This takes us back once more to the meaning of "justification." Earlier we equated it with the forgiveness of sins. Along with that basic and underlying definition, justification literally has the idea of "declaring righteous." It has its background in the language of a court of law. Apart from God we are guilty as accused by the Law, yet Jesus takes our "conviction" and rightful "sentence" upon Himself. He assumes our obligation under the Law, and in addition assumes our penalty for having fallen short of the Law's comprehensive standards. At the same time we have His righteousness given to us. Thus we have been "pardoned," "acquitted," or declared "not guilty" before God. The debt and penalty have been paid.

The pardon and acquittal—the "blessed exchange"—can take place only because Jesus did not remain in the grave but was raised from the dead on Easter morning. The significance and absolute necessity of the resurrection comes through when we read that "[Jesus] was delivered over to death for our sins and was raised to life for our justification" (Romans 4:25).

What, precisely, does Jesus' resurrection mean? First of all, the resurrection confirms Jesus' claim to be the very Son of God, for it demonstrates in an unmistakable way the Savior's conquest of death (Romans 1:4).

The resurrection of Jesus certifies and seals the victory won on the cross for us. To the outside observer, the crucifixion of Jesus must have appeared to be total defeat and humiliation. But, viewed in the light of events occurring three days later, we see the cross not only as an instrument of death but as a necessary step leading ultimately to victory and life. The resurrection of Jesus Christ is God's great reversal of the work of death.

The fact that the Redeemer and Reconciler could not be contained by the grave means that He can be present to comfort and help us today. In addition, the New Testament indicates over and over again that the resurrection of Jesus is a prelude of events to come, events we can and should anticipate with great joy. Jesus' resurrection is a promise of *our* resurrection through Him. St. Paul explains the connection this way:

But Christ has indeed been raised from the dead,
the firstfruits of those who have fallen asleep. For
since death came through a man, the resurrection of
the dead comes also through a man. For as in Adam
all die, so in Christ all will be made alive. But each
in his own turn: Christ, the firstfruits; then, when
He comes, those who belong to Him. (1 Corinthians
15:20–23)

In this way we can say that the "new age"—eternity, really—has already begun. How? Because we are living today in the interval of time between Jesus' resurrection and our own. Since He has risen from the dead, eternal life is not merely possible or even probable for us. Rather, it has already begun, as God "in His great mercy He has given us new birth into a living hope through the resurrection of Jesus Christ from the dead, and into an inheritance that can never perish, spoil or fade—kept in heaven for you" (1 Peter 1:3–4).

The crucifixion of Jesus Christ in our place and His resurrection has occupied a great deal of our attention thus far. This is only fitting when we remember that the apostle Paul identified Christ's death for our sins and His resurrection on the third day as "of first importance" (1 Corinthians 15:3). The justification we discussed earlier—that is, our forgiveness, acquittal, and pardon—can only come about through Jesus' death as our substitute and His resurrection to new life. There is no other way.

As our substitute Jesus satisfied all of the demands of the righteous and holy God against humankind.

The Work of Christ

Theologians use the term "vicarious" for this substitutionary work of Christ. Jesus reconciled the world to God (see 2 Corinthians 5:19) and completed the "atonement" (sometimes theologically divided as "at-onement"). This reconciliation is perfect. God is fully reconciled to all people and nothing more needs to be done. There are no outstanding obligations. Also, this reconciliation is complete or universal, which means that the triune God is fully reconciled to all people without exception. No one is left out.

Lutheran theology uses the term "objective" or "universal" justification for this important truth. It means very simply that on the basis of the completed work of Jesus Christ, God has declared that the world is justified and that all sins have been forgiven.

Taught clearly in such passages as 2 Corinthians 5:19 and Romans 5:15, this form of justification is "objective" because it is God's act of mercy that takes place before we respond to it. Our response does not in some way cause God to be gracious. He is gracious and has already demonstrated the depths of His grace by sending His Son into our world and laying our sin upon Him. We call this form of justification "universal" because everybody is included in the verdict. When Jesus declared, "It is finished" (John 19:30), the penalty for all the sins of every human being had been paid—including the sins of people who have wronged us and whom we find so hard to forgive.

True, in the last analysis there are some who are condemned and lost eternally. However, this is not on account of any outstanding or unpardoned sin, but rather by their unbelief they have arrogantly refused God's gift of forgiveness. This refusal to claim the gift does not destroy the gift. But the gift becomes of no use to the refuser.

For God did not send His Son into the world to con-
demn the world, but to save the world through Him.
Whoever believes in Him is not condemned, but
whoever does not believe stands condemned already
because he has not believed in the name of God's
one and only Son. (John 3:17–18)

Distinctly Different

So far we have focused on the grace of God and the work of Jesus Christ on our behalf as that which accomplishes our justification and secures for us the forgiveness of sins. This is only proper, for nothing other than the mercy of God for the sake of Jesus Christ can win salvation for us.

Perhaps, more than anything else, this insistence that forgiveness comes by grace alone has been *the* distinguishing feature of Lutheran Christianity. None of our own works or efforts, however well-intended they might be, dare ever be credited with winning God's favor. "For it is by grace you have been saved, through faith—and this not from yourselves, it is the gift of God—not by works, so that no one can boast" (Ephesians 2:8–9). When we talk about the righteousness by which we stand before God, certain of His pardon, this is the righteousness He gives to us in the Gospel. "For in the gospel a righteousness from God is revealed" (Romans 1:17).

The moment we say that God's mercy depends on or is a response to some act we perform, our forgiveness becomes uncertain. Why? Because we can never be sure that what we have done is good enough or complete enough. Even more fundamentally, even our best efforts are still tainted by the disease of sin that afflicts all of us. The Christian Gospel states that from beginning to end salvation is totally the work of God in Jesus Christ.

When one stops to think about it, this Gospel fact is a source of great comfort. No matter what we might have done—and no matter how many times we may have done "it"—God's mercy and forgiveness remain there for us. We cannot cancel or otherwise abolish God's grace. Certainly this does not mean that we should continue a sinful pattern of life; we ought not "go on sinning so that grace may increase" (Romans

6:1). The Gospel is not an excuse to keep sinning. On the contrary, when properly understood, the Gospel motivates us and makes it possible for us to lead God-pleasing lives. The apostle Paul notes, "Those who belong to Christ Jesus have crucified the sinful nature with its passions and desires" (Galatians 5:24).

But where do people enter the picture? How do we respond? The New Testament provides a clear answer to this question: The same forgiveness won by Jesus Christ is personally received through faith alone.

What Is Faith?

At its most basic level, faith is the trust and confidence that Jesus is our Savior and that He has obtained for us forgiveness of our sins. When a person lays hold of Jesus as his or her Savior through God-given faith, Lutheran theology has traditionally called this "subjective justification."

We need to be very clear that faith is not a conviction we ourselves generate. As noted earlier, on our own we are altogether "dead in transgressions." We cannot bring ourselves back to spiritual life. We have to be "born again." This takes place when the Holy Spirit creates faith in our hearts.

The Spirit gives us new life in Jesus Christ. Indeed, "No one can say, 'Jesus is Lord,' except by the Holy Spirit" (1 Corinthians 12:3). When the Holy Spirit produces this confidence or trust in us—whether through "the washing of rebirth and renewal" (Titus 3:5) that takes place in Baptism or through the proclamation of the Gospel message itself (Romans 10:17)—then we can be sure that we have been "born again."

There are a lot of Christians who talk about making a decision for Christ and pinpointing an exact time or situation when they first believed. They talk about being "born again" and may challenge us in terms of our own faith. But the question "Are you born again?" need not trouble you. Really it is just another way of asking whether you trust Jesus Christ as your Savior from sin. An affirmative answer is a sure indication that you have indeed been "born again."

When one is brought to faith by the Holy Spirit, he or she has been converted, or regenerated (born again). We are thus justified by grace, for Christ's sake, through faith. In this sequence faith is the instrument through which we claim for ourselves the forgiveness gained for all people by Jesus Christ. We must reassert once more a very important point: God does not declare us righteous and adopt us as His own again as a "reward" for our believing. That would make us at least partially responsible for our salvation and would destroy the consistent New Testament teaching that we are justified by grace *alone.*

The emphasis is always on God's giving: therefore, faith is the empty hand that receives Christ's forgiveness and claims God's promise. Lutherans have summarized all of this by stating that "faith justifies" solely and exclusively because of its object, Jesus Christ.

We hasten to add that our certainty of salvation never rests on our feelings at the moment, on whether we are confident or momentarily unsure. In times of doubt and insecurity, the only safe counsel is to direct our eyes away from ourselves and away from our own emotions. Indeed, when we are troubled by our position in the sight of God, the place to which we should look is the face of Jesus Christ, whom Martin Luther described as a "mirror of the Father's heart." Our gaze should be fixed firmly and immovably on the cross and empty tomb of Jesus, for nothing can undo or take away what was gained for us there. "If you confess with your mouth, 'Jesus is Lord,' and believe in your heart that God raised Him from the dead, you will be saved" (Romans 10:9). Note the Bible doesn't say you have to "feel" saved.

When we are born to a new life in Jesus Christ, our old sinful life dies.

*Don't you know that all of us who were baptized
into Christ Jesus were baptized into His death? We
were therefore buried with Him through baptism
into death in order that, just as Christ was raised
from the dead through the glory of the Father, we
too may live a new life. (Romans 6:3–4)*

Practically speaking, this means that we no longer live for ourselves in pursuit of our own ambitions. Rather, we draw our life from God and seek to serve Him. The good works that we do are not good in and of themselves. They are good because they are motivated by the Gospel and are performed in faith. God is now working in and through us for others. This is why good works are often referred to as the fruit of faith, since they are a spontaneous, natural response to the gift of God's forgiveness. Above all, we do not perform good works in order to gain God's approval. Such approval is a free gift of grace realized in Jesus Christ.

One final comment is in order. God's forgiveness given by grace for the sake of Jesus Christ is not only vital at the beginning of a person's spiritual life, but it is absolutely indispensable throughout the course of one's spiritual existence as well. There is never a moment when we can stand before God deserving His favor or claiming anything from Him as rightfully our own. The only thing we ever "deserve" is condemnation, for "in the sinful nature [I am] a slave to the law of sin" (Romans 7:25). We can stand confidently before God because He has outfitted us in the righteousness of Jesus Christ, so that when God looks at us He does not see the sin clinging to us, intruding into everything that even Christian people attempt. Rather, He sees the benefits of Christ that He Himself gives us out of His own mercy. The apostle Paul draws this together splendidly, picking up on the thought begun in the verse quoted above:

*Therefore, there is now no condemnation for those
who are in Christ Jesus, because through Christ
Jesus the law of the Spirit of life set me free from the*

law of sin and death. For what the law was power-
less to do in that it was weakened by the sinful
nature, God did by sending His own Son in the like-
ness of sinful man to be a sin offering. And so He
condemned sin in sinful man, in order that the
righteous requirements of the law might be fully met
in us, who do not live according to the sinful nature
but according to the Spirit. (Romans 8:1–4)

We stand before God as His forgiven sons and daughters by grace alone, for Christ's sake alone, through faith alone—from start to finish.

The theme of these pages has been the forgiveness of sins, coming to us as a free gift of God's mercy and obtained for us by the life, death, and resurrection of our substitute, Jesus Christ. To top it off, God's Spirit gives us the faith to trust in this promised forgiveness. This is the Gospel proclaimed so clearly throughout the Bible. "For God so loved the world that He gave His one and only Son, that whoever believes in Him shall not perish but have eternal life" (John 3:16).

As noted at the outset, there are many different ways of describing the reality of this forgiveness. Examples of these terms are "redemption," "reconciliation," "covenant," and many more. Lutheran theology has traditionally emphasized the term "justification," following the example of St. Paul in particular, but in doing so, we have not overlooked the extraordinarily rich variety of interrelated concepts used by Scripture to communicate the same magnificent truth.

The one overriding truth is that God has taken the initiative to restore His thoroughly fallen creatures to Himself, and He went to such lengths that He would sacrifice His own Son to accomplish the rescue. Everything else relates to this Gospel affirmation and derives its meaning from it. It is the core, or essence, of Christianity, so much so that Lutheran theology has—without any fear of overstatement—flatly declared it to be "the article by which the church stands or falls."

Discussion Questions

Why can "rescue" be said to be the theme of the entire Bible?

Do you, as a Christian, feel rescued? How? When? Why?

What is grace? Where does it come from?

Why is Christ's resurrection crucial to the matter of justification and rescue?

What does the concept of "objective" or "universal" justification mean to you?

Is there anything you can do to earn or assure your salvation?

What is faith? Where does it come from?

How do you know you have faith? How do you respond to it?

5

Sanctification

BY DEAN WENTHE

In his book The Fellowship of the Ring, J. R. R. Tolkien provides a colorful description of the hobbits. Tolkien tells of their bare feet, bright colors, and broad cheeks. You could easily identify hobbits if you were to encounter one because of Tolkien's detailed descriptions.

What if you were asked to provide a description of a Christian? What traits would you list? Are there any aspects of a Christian's appearance that could tip others off? How about young Christians? Do they wear different clothing? listen to different music? Are they, like hobbits, "bright-eyed, red-cheeked, with mouths apt to laughter"?

One way this question has been answered is to rehearse all the actions that a young Christian *doesn't* do, at least when he or she acts in character. The Christian, we're told, "*doesn't* swear, *doesn't* steal, *doesn't* curse, *doesn't* covet, *doesn't* this, and *doesn't* that . . ."

The problem with this answer is that it leaves the impression that the Christian, unlike the hobbit, has little to laugh about. Rather, the Christian life must be spent avoiding avenues and actions that might lead to an infraction of the rules.

Is there a better way to describe how a Christian can be distinguished from others? Can we describe what a Christian *does* do rather than only what he or she *doesn't* do? Can we present the positive rather than the negative?

Perhaps the most positive proposal in all of the world is precisely the departure point for our answer. "You shall have no other gods before

Me" (Exodus 20:3).

Luther explained that this means Christians "fear, love, and trust in God above all things." Letting God be God is the most positive step that any human being can take! This step, when it begins a lifelong walk with God, is the one way to fun and fulfillment that lasts.

St. Paul had tried his best to find some satisfaction in the negatives: don't swear, don't steal, and so forth. His day was filled with prophets who fashioned such negatives. "To be religious," they argued, "is to be conformed to these negatives."

But then Paul's perspective was reversed by that explosively positive voice, "I am Jesus" (Acts 9:5).

The moment Paul knew that it was the great God of Israel who was present in the voice of Jesus, his knowledge of the positive expanded. Suddenly there were many things *to do*, not just bad things which one should *not do*.

> Rejoice in the Lord always. I will say it again:
> Rejoice! . . . Whatever is true, whatever is noble,
> whatever is right, whatever is pure, whatever is
> lovely, whatever is admirable—if anything is excel-
> lent or praiseworthy—think about such things.
> (Philippians 4:4, 8)

A touchdown. A tennis match. A camping trip. A computer. Good food. Faithful friends. A fascinating book. Fashionable clothing. Fine art. A Christian may enjoy and savor these and countless others of life's pleasures. The Christian rejoices in the blessings of God.

Our lives as followers of Jesus are not marked by conformity, as though Christ were a drill sergeant forcing rules upon us and marching us in monotonous formation. Far from this! Christ has opened up the infinite variety of God's creation for our pleasure. He provides new possibilities and permits us to be as different as His first disciples. Think of

Peter, James, and John; Martha and Mary; Moses and Miriam. How different they were in appearance and attitude! How splendid was the manner in which God showered His love across the full spectrum of their personalities!

Whether young or old, rich or poor, Christians share a common trait that marks them as a people set apart—unique—radically different from the decaying universe in which they live. They are committed to "letting God be God." His love reaches and teaches them; God's people listen to the same voice St. Paul heard saying, "I am Jesus." They respond to that voice in love and reach out to others. This is the positive portrait that Christians can confidently exhibit.

You can see this portrait! In Baptism, where Jesus speaks His forgiving Word, a new Christian being is formed. In the Lord's Supper, where the bread of life is offered, that new life is nourished. In Sacred Scripture, where the face of a faithful Savior satisfies our deepest longing for a life that can be free of sin's constricting conformity, guidance is given.

Paul knew perfectly well how the negatives could enclose humanity. The day-to-day fruit of such old soil is all too familiar to each of us. Even accompanied by electric guitar and amplified by great speakers, it's the same old, stale song that has moved mankind too long. It's obvious stuff, if we step back and reflect a moment.

> *The acts of the sinful nature are obvious: sexual immorality, impurity and debauchery; idolatry and witchcraft; hatred, discord, jealously, fits of rage, selfish ambition, dissensions, factions and envy; drunkenness, orgies, and the like. (Galatians 5:19–21)*

Things are like that! The Christian, particularly the young Christian, can immediately see the bland conformity of many who think they're doing something "new." Sin is a "look-alike" affair. It makes its victims into mannequins who can only mimic what some satanic master suggests.

The tragedy is that things don't have to be like that! Our lives can escape the old rut that offers only worn-out songs! Christ's life presents a positive departure from such dead ends! His life, His work on Calvary, His resurrection and ascension, destroy the dungeons in which our lives are so easily encased.

Christians are free to live for a God who has revealed His innermost sentiments on the cross of Calvary! God's sentiments are to save lives from that deep pit of monotony into which they inevitably descend due to their own dark selfishness.

By letting God be God, some remarkably new adventures are in store for us. The Holy Spirit will provide concrete contours to our character. "But the fruit of the Spirit is love, joy, peace, patience, kindness, goodness, faithfulness, gentleness and self-control" (Galatians 5:22–23).

The beauty of the Spirit's work in us is that it produces such rich and varied fruits. The sorts of clothing we wear, the types of movies we attend, the sports and hobbies we pursue: these can be as different as night and day. The Christian teenager knows that there is no straight-jacket of negatives to numb life and constrict "really living." Cultic fanaticism, crass faddism, and canned conformity are seen for what they are: a flattening of God's good creation into the evil confinement of look-alike sin and frustration.

Hatred and jealousy, however justifiable, are not attractive. Drunkenness, whether drug- or alcohol-induced, is not appealing. Promiscuity and pornographic abuse of sexuality are not appropriate. The Christian strives to avoid these because God forbids them, to be sure. However, these are not just rules to keep a person from a good time. Rather, God has a positive design for lives that such rules enhance.

The Christian teenager can celebrate the fact that God has provided the criteria for true fun and a happy life. The joys of genuine love, the pleasures of good food and drink. The fulfillment of a marriage marked by fidelity. Friendship that endures. These are great and good things! An unbeliever may enjoy the gifts, but the Christian can truly appreciate the gifts because he knows the Giver.

Our confession of failure in prayer is speedily answered. Our request that God refresh us with His mercy in Christ puts us back on the track. To get stuck in the ruts of that old conformity is now as unnatural for us as it would be for the hobbit to suddenly lose his fondness for yellow and green. Our fondness for God—our response to that great positive "You shall"—has given us a new perspective for living.

We now know that "letting God be God" also lets us be ourselves. As surely as an apple tree produces apples, Christians will produce those fruits of "love, joy, peace . . ." that can grow only in baptized soil.

The fact that such fruits are surrounded by produce of a very different sort does not surprise us. Our old nature continually tries to plant the sour seeds of sin where they don't belong. The Ten Commandments warn us about the seeds that are incompatible with our Christian soil. They are not, therefore, great negatives that make sin look all the more attractive (like the boy who always thought the apples across the fence were more delicious).

The Ten Commandments are more like the "poison" label on certain containers. The "skull and crossbones" sign alerts us that the ingredients are not compatible with our chemistry. To eat or to drink such a commodity can cause illness and even death. To ignore the Ten Commandments creates a grave danger to our Christian character. A critical level of toxins is also life-threatening in spiritual matters.

The tonic for our souls, the medicine for our deepest disease, and the water that really quenches our thirst is the person of Jesus Christ. His character defines who we are. His life shows us how we are to live. His suffering shows us how we are to serve. His love and forgiveness renews us each day. His death and resurrection even shows us what our dying and rising will be.

So our paragraph on what the Christian is like will be positive! It will point to Jesus Christ! Real Christians have the character of Christ even as imaginary hobbits have their traits. Because the character of Christ is for real and for them, Christians have more reasons than hobbits to "laugh, often and heartily." Life is a celebration!

Discussion Questions

Describe a Christian.

What common trait marks all Christians and sets them apart from everybody else?

What is "confession" and "absolution"?
Why is it important for our sanctified living?

Why/how is the Christian life different from and better than a worldly life?

How has God provided for "true fun"?

Where can you stand improvement in your own life?

Where and how can the Holy Spirit build your life?

6

One God in Three Persons

BY WILLIAM WEINRICH

𝒢𝓁𝑜𝓇𝓎 𝒷𝑒 𝓉𝑜 𝓉𝒽𝑒 𝐹𝑎𝓉𝒽𝑒𝓇 and to the Son and to the Holy Spirit; as it was in the beginning, is now, and will be forever. Amen.

Has anyone ever asked you the question "Do you believe in God?" If so, you probably answered, "Yes, I do believe in God." The person asking such a question may really be asking something like this: "Do you believe that there is a mighty being who created the world?" or "Do you believe that there is a mighty supreme being who now somehow is controlling the world?" or perhaps "Do you believe that there is a being who has given to us absolute moral rules?"

When you answer these questions about belief in God with a "Yes," do you have other questions in mind? Very likely you do—and there is nothing wrong with that.

There are many people who "believe in god" in the way these questions suggest. People of the Jewish faith "believe in god"; people of the Islamic faith "believe in god." Indeed, many people of no specific religion at all "believe in god." Did you ever stop to think that people can "believe in god" without really believing in God at all?

Perhaps we need to ask this question: "Do you believe in God the Father, God the Son, and God the Holy Spirit?" or, more simply, "Do you believe in the Trinity?" This question asks whether one believes in God as the Christians believe in Him. The view of the one God as a "trinity" is the distinctively Christian view of God. Why is this so? What is so Christian about the doctrine of the Trinity? What is so important about it for our Christian faith and life? Why is the idea of God as Trinity more than just a difficult abstraction?

Often Christians think of the Trinity as a strange and difficult idea that, in the last analysis, has little if any importance for our faith. However, the confession that God is a Trinity has very definite relation to our confession that Jesus is Savior and Lord. We may even say that Christians confess that God is Trinity because they confess that Jesus is Savior and Lord. God, precisely as the one God who is Trinity, is the God of the Gospel.

"I believe in one God" (Nicene Creed). The Bible makes no clearer affirmation than that there is one God. "Monotheism" is the term we use to refer to the belief that there is only one God. Both the Old Testament and the New Testament exhibit a strong monotheistic viewpoint. There is only one God who exists; everything else is a creature that exists only because the one God created it. Only the one God exists in Himself, that is, receives His existence and life from no other. The prophet Isaiah is typical of this central biblical belief: "This is what the LORD says, Israel's King and Redeemer, the LORD Almighty: I am the first and I am the last; apart from Me there is no God" (Isaiah 44:6).

Since there is but one God, everything else that is worshiped as God is in fact an empty idol. Isaiah mercilessly satirizes the dead, power-less idols of his pagan neighbors (Isaiah 44:9–20). Of course, in our day we usually do not have idols made of wood or of stone, and we do not pray to such things as though they were alive and heard us. Nonetheless, many people place their trust and hope in material things and fall into despair if they happen to lose it all. It is not uncommon to find young people and adults who believe that physical vitality and a well-paying job are necessary ingredients for a happy life. We hear from time to time of those who lose their jobs and become so despondent that they take their own life. Such tragic and unhappy persons have fallen to an idolatry of things.

Equally destructive is the flight to alcohol or drugs as an escape from the struggles of daily life. In these and in many other not so tragic ways, people in our own day place their trust and hope in things other than in the one God, who alone can grant life's blessings and support. But the Bible says, "You shall have no other gods before Me" (Exodus 20:3). Because we, too, are subject to the failures and disappointments of life, we should always pray that God will keep us faithful to Himself and free from the false and deceptive trust in false gods.

One, Eternal God

Why is it so important that we confess one God and place our trust and hope only in Him? Three reasons immediately come to mind.

* *The Bible repeatedly asserts that there is only one God. "The LORD is God; besides Him there is no other" (Deuteronomy 4:35). The New Testament witnesses to the same conviction. (See 1 Corinthians 8:6; James 2:19.) Monotheism is, therefore, the basis of the Bible's teaching concerning God.*

* *Often the Bible speaks of God as our Creator and our Redeemer (Isaiah 44:6, 24). The Bible proclaims the true source of our life and indeed of all good things. To trust in any other thing or in any other person will ultimately lead to frustration and disappointment. Only God can provide the necessities for a good and contented life, and He alone can give us salvation and eternal life. No one else can give us these things; only God can. Belief in one God, therefore, points us realistically to the true source of our life and of all those things that will give us fullness and worth.*

* *The Bible also speaks of the one God as the God of promise. (Read Deuteronomy 6:4–19.) God promises that if we cling to Him in faith He will indeed give us the fullness of His blessings. That there*

is one God, therefore, is related to our hope in God. The fact that there is one God provides the foundation for our hope that He who promised us eternal blessings can make good on His promises.

Suppose for a moment that there is another god of equal strength and might. Were that the case, then the will of God to grant us His blessings would be subject to the veto of the other. God's will could always be hindered or even thwarted by the other god. Were there another god, the God of promise might, in fact, never be able to keep His promises. It would be like a heavenly tug-of-war between two equally strong men, each trying to pull the other into the ditch, yet because of the equal strength never being able to do so. We would have an eternal tie, no winner.

But since we confess our belief in one God, we also hope in His promises and trust Him to make good on His promises. Since there is no other god to hinder or to thwart Him, the one God can do as He promised. Since His will to fulfill His promises cannot be countered, the one God will act on the promises He has made.

The Bible does not simply speak of God as "one." It speaks of God as a person. God is not like an abstract mathematical unit that is singular and stands alone. We do not speak of God as an "it." We use a personal pronoun and speak of God as "He." The reason for this is that the Bible always speaks of God as a personal subject, as one who is in relation to another. God keeps His promises. He is merciful. He sees and hears His people (Exodus 3:7–8). He speaks and teaches (Deuteronomy 6:1). He loves (John 3:16). God can be angry (Deuteronomy 9:8, 19–20, 22). God can be long-suffering and patient (1 Peter 3:20). "Its" are none of those things.

All of these things would be impossible were there not someone to whom God was relating. For example, one cannot be merciful unless there is someone else toward whom one is merciful. One cannot be patient unless there is someone with whom one is patient. The Bible always presents God as one who is actively engaged with another, whether that be with His chosen people or with His enemies. The Bible never presents God as one who is uninterested and detached. God is not like an absentee landlord who simply owns the property but is never involved in its upkeep and improvement. The Bible always presents God as one who is speaking and acting, that is, as one who is actively engaged with someone else.

Before the Beginning

Since the Bible begins with the story of the creation of the world and with the story of mankind's fall into sin, the Bible usually presents God speaking and relating to the world, to men and women.

But now let us ask this question—what about before the world was created? Was God also personal then? Or did God become personal only when He created the world? If God only became personal and only began to relate to another when He created the world, that would mean that God was not personal before the world was created. God Himself apart from the world would not be a personal being.

However, that is not the picture of God the Bible gives. It is a part of God's nature to always relate to another. A relationship with another is part of God's nature. But that implies that even before the creation of the world God was personal. Even before the creation of the world God was in relationship. But if there is only one God, as we have seen, with whom was God relating before the world existed? With whom was God speaking before the creation of the world?

The answer to these questions is given already at the beginning of the Bible in the creation account. "Then God said, 'Let Us make man in Our image'" (Genesis 1:26). God is Himself not singular and unitary. He is Himself a community of persons who stand in relationship with one another.

The Bible designates this community of persons with the names "Father," "Son," and "Holy Spirit." To be sure, the trinitarian nature of God is a mystery, and it is impossible to truly understand with our finite minds. Yet, the truth that God is a community of persons is extremely important for our faith, for we are assured that when God speaks to us and relates to us, it is not an "unnatural" thing for Him to do. When God addresses mankind and comes into communion with mankind, God is acting in such a way that reveals Him and makes Him known.

When we say that it is "natural" for God to speak to man, that it is "natural" for God to come into communion with man, we are saying something about God Himself. We are not saying that God simply chose to speak to man. He could just as simply not have spoken to man. Rather we are saying that it is a part of God's own "nature" that He speaks and communes with man. For this reason we confess God to be a community of persons. Moreover, this community of persons is characterized by love, for as John says, "God is love" (1 John 4:8). It is "natural" to God that He speak to mankind in love and that He act for the benefit of mankind.

The Nature of God

Have you ever acted in such a way that others said to you, "You're not yourself today." Perhaps you were tired, cranky, or just generally obnoxious. Your parents or friends remarked that something must have happened to make you behave differently than you normally behave. Of course, the opposite can also be the case. There are persons who are usually so unfriendly and quarrelsome that when they are nice we wonder, What happened to make him (or her) so friendly today? Implied in both cases is the recognition that certain actions are "true" to the person who does them, while other actions do not correspond to the real character, or nature, of that person.

It is through someone's actions that are "true" to the person that we come to know that person. We know a person to be friendly because that person acts in a friendly way. We know a person to be trustworthy because that person acts in a trustworthy way. We never really come to know a person except in those ways in which a person presents himself to us. A friend can say to us, "You're not yourself today" because that friend knows us.

Often the Bible, especially the Psalms, includes prayers that ask God to act in such and such a way. Some of these prayers speak of God's mercy and love, that is, of God and Savior:

> *Do not withhold Your mercy from me, O LORD;*
> *may Your love and Your truth always protect me.*
> *(Psalm 40:11)*

> *Have mercy on me, O God, according to Your*
> *unfailing love; according to Your great compassion*
> *blot out my transgressions. (Psalm 51:1)*

> *Save me, O God, by Your name; vindicate me by*
> *Your might. (Psalm 54:1)*

> *Show us Your unfailing love, O LORD, and grant us*
> *Your salvation. (Psalm 85:7)*

On other occasions, however, the Bible speaks of God's anger and judgment:

> *Break the arm of the wicked and evil man; call him*
> *to account for his wickedness that would not be*
> *found out. (Psalm 10:15)*

> *O LORD God Almighty, the God of Israel, rouse*

Yourself to punish all the nations; show no mercy to
wicked traitors. (Psalm 59:5)

O LORD God Almighty, how long will Your anger
smolder against the prayers of Your people? (Psalm
80:4)

Now, how do you think God would prefer to deal with people? In love? Or in condemning? Both salvation and judgment are, of course, works of God. God can and does save; and He can and does condemn. But in which action is He more like Himself? And in which is God acting because something happened to make Him act that way?

God looks down from heaven on the sons of men to
see if there are any who understand, any who seek
God. Everyone has turned away, they have together
become corrupt; there is no one who does good, not
even one. . . . There they were, overwhelmed with
dread, where there was nothing to dread. God scat-
tered the bones of those who attacked you; you put
them to shame, for God despised them. (Psalm
53:2–3, 5)

Clearly, because men have rejected God—God punishes and condemns them. Repeatedly in the Psalms, in the prophets, indeed, throughout the Bible man's sin is shown to be the cause of God's judgment and wrath. For example, Ezekiel prophesies that "because they had shed blood in the land and because they had defiled it with their idols" (Ezekiel 36:18), God poured out His wrath upon the people and scattered them among the nations. Think also of the story of man's fall into sin. Because Adam and Eve sinned, God put them out of Eden.

"God is love" (1 John 4:8). When God acts in anger and wrath as the Judge, therefore, He is not acting in a way "true" to Himself. He is angry because of man's sin and evil. The cause of God's anger originates outside of God. God is not, by nature, an angry god.

Restore us again, O God our Savior, and put away
Your displeasure toward us. Will You be angry with
us forever? Will You prolong Your anger through all
generations? Will You not revive us again, that Your
people may rejoice in You? Show us Your unfailing
love, O LORD, and grant us Your salvation. (Psalm
85:4–7)

The psalmist appeals for God's unfailing love, for he knows that God's indignation and anger are not the way God would like to act. Rather, the psalmist asks God to be compassionate toward His people: "Show us Your unfailing love." In Psalm 86 David says, "But You, O Lord, are a compassionate and gracious God, slow to anger, abounding in love and faithfulness" (Psalm 86:15).

It is characteristic of God to be merciful, to love. The cause of God's love and mercy does not originate outside of God. Rather, God is Himself the cause of His mercy and love. In fact, when the Bible speaks of God acting "righteously," it often means that God is acting in accordance with Himself, according to His own nature. God is righteous when He is "being Himself." And for that reason, God's righteousness is often connected with the Gospel. "I am not ashamed of the gospel, because it is the power of God for the salvation of everyone who believes. . . . For in the gospel a righteousness from God is revealed" (Romans 1:16–17).

Because it is God's nature to be merciful and to love, we say that we are saved by the grace of God without any merit in us. God's love and mercy have their cause in God Himself. Nothing outside of God causes God to be merciful or to love. When God acts in love and mercy, He is acting by grace, out of Himself alone.

According to the New Testament, it is Jesus of Nazareth who is the complete and true reply to the prayer of the psalmist, "Show us Your unfailing love." Jesus is the very expression of the love of God. "This is how God showed His love among us: He sent His one and only Son into the world that we might live through Him. This is love: not that we loved God, but that He loved us and sent His Son as an atoning sacrifice for our sins" (1 John 4:9–10). God is Himself in the life and death of Jesus. In Jesus we come to know God as He is.

In His life and death Jesus reveals God, who is love. But reflect again on the words of the apostle John in 1 John 4:9. It does not say that God's love began with the sending of the Son. It says that God's love was shown to us in Christ. His love is revealed in Jesus. This implies that God's love existed before the sending of the Son.

Earlier we noted that to be personal meant to be in relation to another. So also with love. One cannot love unless there is a recipient of that love. If, as John says, God is love (1 John 4:8), that means that within God there is a relationship of love, a lover and a beloved. And indeed that is what Jesus is talking about when He spoke of the Father's love: "You loved Me before the creation of the world" (John 17:24).

God did not first begin to love when the world and mankind were created. Mankind was not the first object of God's affection. Rather, God's Son was the object of the Father's love. Since the Father is God, who is eternal, and since the Son is God, who is eternal, this love of the Father for the Son is not simply an action, a happening, a temporary affection within God. This love of the Father for the Son is of God; it is eternal and characterizes God Himself.

It is also important to understand that the love of God is not simply an emotion. Rather, divine love includes giving of one's self to another for the purpose and goal of communion and unity. Love demands a relationship between persons. It is this movement of the Father to the Son and the return movement of the Son to the Father; it is the mutual finding of oneself in the other that is in mind when we say, "God is love." "Anyone who has seen Me has seen the Father. . . . Don't you believe that I am in the Father, and that the Father is in Me?" (John 14:9–10).

We read in John's Gospel, "For God so loved the world that He gave His one and only Son" (John 3:16), or in Ephesians, "God, who is rich in mercy, made us alive with Christ even when we were dead in transgressions—it is by grace you have been saved" (Ephesians 2:4–5). Perhaps we can now begin to see the full depth of what is being said.

The love God has for the world in Christ is, if you will, the external expression of the external love the Father has for the Son. "This is how God showed His love among us: He sent His one and only Son into the world that we might live through Him" (1 John 4:9). "As the Father has loved Me, so have I loved you. Now remain in My love" (John 15:9).

Therefore, when we are "in Christ," as Paul often puts it, we are ourselves the objects of the Father's eternal love. Jesus says it this way:

> *I in them and You in Me. May they be brought to*
> *complete unity to let the world know that You sent*
> *Me and have loved them even as You have loved*
> *Me. (John 17:23)*

Therefore, the Gospel of Jesus is the Gospel of the self-giving love of God. The Gospel is not rooted in a temporary decision of the divine will or in history. It is not rooted in ourselves or in anything that is changeable and temporary. Rather, the Gospel of Jesus is rooted in God Himself.

When the proclamation, therefore, comes—"Believe on the Lord Jesus Christ and you shall be saved"—it says, in effect, "You can stake your life and destiny on Jesus, for He is Himself God from God. What He did on the cross for you is the very outpouring of the Father's eternal love for the Son. Clinging fast in faith, trust, and hope to Jesus, the incarnate Son of the Father, we have the Father's own eternal love. In the Son we have communion with the Father!" Our salvation is as sure and firm as God Himself is sure and firm.

> *For I am convinced that neither death nor life, nei-*
> *ther angels nor demons, neither the present nor the*
> *future, nor any powers, neither height nor depth,*
> *nor anything else in all creation, will be able to sep-*
> *arate us from the love of God that is in Christ Jesus*
> *our Lord. (Romans 8:38–39)*

The love of Jesus for the sinner is the expression of the Father's eternal love for the Son. This love of the eternal Father for the eternal Son is then itself eternal and will never pass away.

The coming of Jesus into the flesh, and His ministry of love even unto death, brings us into the eternal relationship of love between the Father and the Son. Being with the Father in Christ, by grace we are given and participate in the divine life. This life is not just unending existence; it is participation in the unity of love between the Father and the Son. John speaks of our love for one another as God's love among us: "If we love one another, God lives in us and His love is made complete in us" (1 John 4:12).

Until now, we have mentioned only the Father and the Son, because in as simple and direct a way as possible we wanted to indicate that God is a unity of persons. However, the Bible repeatedly mentions a third divine person along with the Father and Son, namely, the Holy Spirit. At creation, the Spirit is "hovering over the waters" (Genesis 1:2). According to Ezekiel, the Spirit is the guiding presence of God bringing about a holy and obedient people (Ezekiel 36:27). Jesus receives the Holy Spirit at His baptism (Matthew 3:16) and is nurtured by the Spirit during His temptation (Matthew 4:1).

The Holy Spirit is the source and power of our new life in Christ (Romans 8:2–11). As the Pentecost story tells us, the Holy Spirit is the power of the life of all the church (Acts 2). Often the Bible simply mentions the Holy Spirit along with the Father and the Son. One thinks especially of Matthew 28:19, which tells us to baptize "in the name of the Father and of the Son and of the Holy Spirit." But we could refer as well to such passages as 1 Corinthians 12:4–11; Ephesians 4:1–7; 1 Peter 1:2; and 1 John 4:13.

In some ways the Holy Spirit can seem the most difficult part of the doctrine of the Trinity. But let us recall again that it is through the works of God that God reveals Himself. God's work is not only the sending of the Son, but also includes giving us new life in Christ, creating a new heart in us, leading us into a new way of obedience, and uniting us in communion with God and with our fellow Christians. This giving and new living in love is God Himself working His way in us and through us.

The Holy Spirit is God giving to us the gift of God the Son, who is given to us by God the Father.

Thus Paul can write, "For through Him [Christ] we both have access to the Father by one Spirit" (Ephesians 2:18). Similarly, the unity of mutual love and peace that Christians experience among themselves and for which they pray to be among themselves is the binding work of the Holy Spirit, in whom we participate in the love of Father and Son. As John puts it, "We know that we live in Him and He in us, because He has given us of His Spirit" (1 John 4:13). Paul exhorts us to "be patient, bearing with one another in love. Make every effort to keep the unity of the Spirit through the bond of peace" (Ephesians 4:2b–3).

The Christian confesses God to be Trinity because the new life in Christ involves a life with others in mutual, self-giving love. This life is one life shared with others. And this is not our life. We do not have this life in ourselves or from ourselves. This life of love with others is a gift; it is the gracious gift of God "being Himself" for us, Father, Son, and Holy Spirit.

Discussion Questions

What is the function of God the Father?

What is the function of God the Son?

What is the function of God the Holy Spirit?

How would you explain God as the Trinity?

Reflect on what makes God different from all the other things man worships as God.

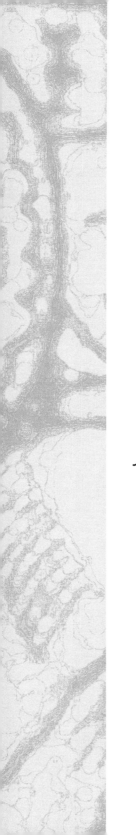

7

Jesus Christ: God for Man and Man for God

BY WILLIAM WEINRICH

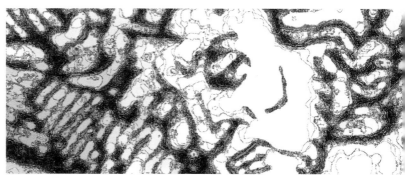

In the beginning was the Word, and the Word was with God, and the Word was God. He was with God in the beginning. Through Him all things were made; without Him nothing was made that has been made. In Him was life, and that life was the light of men. . . . The Word became flesh and made His dwelling among us. We have seen His glory, the glory of the One and Only, who came from the Father, full of grace and truth. . . . From the fullness of His grace we have all received one blessing after another. (John 1:1–4, 14, 16)

I believe that Jesus Christ, true God, begotten of the Father from eternity, and also true man, born of the Virgin Mary, is my Lord, who has redeemed me, a lost and condemned person, purchased and won me from all sins, from death, and from the power of the devil; not with gold or silver, but with His holy, precious blood and with His innocent suffering and death, that I may be His own and live under Him in His kingdom and serve Him in everlasting righteousness, innocence, and blessedness, just as He is risen from the dead, lives and reigns to all eternity. (Explanation of the Second Article of the Apostles' Creed)

Who Is Jesus Christ?

There can be no more central question. Indeed, people were discussing this issue already when Jesus lived. He even asked His disciples, "Who do people say I am?" (Mark 8:27). Through the centuries—down to today—many answers have been offered to that question. For some Jesus is understood primarily as a friend—a companion—present when we need aid and comfort. Others regard Jesus as a source of power in their lives. Still others think Jesus was simply a great moral teacher. In some countries Jesus is regarded as a great example of political or social protest against injustice and oppression. However, these answers are not sufficient in answering the question "Who is Jesus Christ?"

In the Gospel of John we receive the answer Scripture gives to our question. John says of Jesus, "the Word became flesh" (John 1:14). Jesus is God become man. To express this we often use "incarnation," which may be roughly translated "en-flesh-ment." The divine Son of God (the Second Person of the Holy Trinity) became flesh. The word *flesh* here means "human," so John's Gospel does not simply say the Word became flesh and blood, but the Word became all that makes a person human.

Jesus was a human person in every way—just like us. The Gospels depict Jesus doing and experiencing ordinary things common to all humans. Jesus was born; He wept; He hungered; He ate; He thirsted; He drank; He slept; He was anxious; He sorrowed; He hoped; He suffered; He died. Jesus was a human person in every sense except He was sinless.

Nonetheless, when John's Gospel says "the Word became flesh," it does not mean that in "becoming" man the Word ceased to be God. Jesus was the Word incarnate, the divine Word in flesh, which means that Jesus was both God and man at the same time. Therefore, when we speak of the "incarnation" of God, we do not mean God changed into man. Rather, the Son of God (or the Word, as John's Gospel calls Him) united with our human nature in such a way that everything Jesus felt, thought, said, did, or willed was both of God and of man. When Jesus spoke, God was speaking and a man was also speaking. When Jesus acted, God was acting and a man was also acting. With Martin Luther we can answer the question "Who is Jesus Christ?" by saying, "Jesus is true God and also true man."

Perhaps nowhere in the Bible is the fact that Jesus is both God and man more beautifully reflected than in the story of Jesus' birth. When the shepherds went to the manger in Bethlehem, they saw a baby wrapped in swaddling clothes. Now, there is nothing more human in weakness and dependence than a baby. Yet the birth of that baby Jesus was announced by the opening of heaven and the singing of angels.

That ordinary, common birth was clearly a birth with a difference. For in that birth heaven itself had become earthly when the Lord of heaven became man. Therefore, the shepherds are told that the baby they are to seek out is none other than Christ the Lord (Luke 2:8–20). Think of it! That little baby was the Lord, who is mightier than the angels who sang of His birth! That little baby lying in a manger was the Lord of heaven, who contains all things and whom nothing contains! That little baby born of woman when Caesar Augustus ruled the Roman Empire was the eternal Son of God, who has no beginning and no ending!

The truly awesome mystery of the incarnation of God is laid out in the narrative simplicity of the Christmas story. God was that baby; God lay in a manger; God was born of the Virgin Mary!

Jesus of Nazareth, about whom we read in the four Gospels, is both true God and true man. He is the Creator of all things and yet one born in time "when Quirinius was governor of Syria" (Luke 2:2). Ponder for a moment this simple statement: "Jesus is true God and also true man." These are stupendous words! We are, of course, expressing a mystery here. How Jesus can be both true God and true man is not a matter we can easily comprehend. We worship Jesus, a man, as our God and Lord. As the apostle Paul says, every knee should bow at the name of Jesus (Philippians 2:9–10).

When we say Jesus is true God and also true man, we do not want to convey the idea that we are compartmentalizing Jesus. Jesus is not God in part and man in part and so together (as it were, by addition) God and man. Jesus is not like a chemical substance that can be broken down into independent and previously existing parts. It may be true, for example, that water can be broken down into two parts hydrogen and one part oxygen, which when put together again produce water. But Jesus is not in any way like that. He is not one part God and one part man, which together make one God-man! Jesus is not a man to whom divinity has been added. Nor is He God to whom humanity has been added. Jesus is fully, completely, and perfectly God; He is also fully, completely, and perfectly a human person.

This remains a mystery of God's immeasurable love towards humankind. Nevertheless, it is a fundamental confession of the Christian faith that the Christ whom we worship as our God and Lord is both true God and true man. It is important that we understand why it is necessary for the Savior to be both God and man.

A Necessity

The answer to the question "Why?" is implied in these words from the Nicene Creed: "for us men and for our salvation." It is by virtue of what Jesus has done "for us" that we worship Him as true God and true man. We believe that Jesus is true God and true man because He has redeemed us, delivered and freed us from sin, death, and the devil that we might live in His kingdom and serve Him in righteousness, innocence, and blessedness.

To know Jesus as true God is to know Jesus as the One who forgives our sins, frees us from the power of the devil, and gives us a life to live in His name. Only God can forgive sins. Only God is powerful enough to overcome the devil. And only God, who has life in Himself, can give life. We worship Jesus as true God, therefore, because we recognize in Him the source of those heavenly gifts we receive through faith: forgiveness, freedom, salvation, God's love, and many more.

However, we also know Jesus as true man. To know Jesus as true man is not merely to know that He had flesh and blood. We confess Jesus as true man because in our place (for us) He perfectly served and obeyed God in all things. In our place He died for the forgiveness of our sins. In our place He received the life, or resurrection, we shall also receive. All people have sinned against God and for that reason have fallen into death and the power of the devil. For us to be redeemed, delivered, and freed, a Savior had to take our place, that is, He had to be true man—just like us.

Let us summarize a little. To be our Lord and Savior, Jesus must be true God and true man. If Jesus is our Savior, then He must be God. Only God, nothing more and nothing less, can be the subject of salvation—that is—the One who saves from sin, death, and the devil.

In a similar way, if Jesus is our Savior, then He must be also true man. It is man, nothing more and nothing less, who is the object of salvation, that is, who is the recipient of God's saving work. It is man, each and every person, who is the sinner. It is man, each and every person, who is subject to the temptations of the devil. It is man, each and every person, who is under the power of death and will, in fact, die. If Jesus is our Savior, He must be truly human even as you and I are human. The Gospel proclaims, "Jesus saves us!" That is the same as to say, "Jesus is true God and also true man."

When we confess Jesus to be true God, we are not only thinking of His status as God. We are not merely thinking of His divine qualities, or characteristics. To be sure, Jesus is God and is and has all that God is and has. Jesus is immortal, eternal, all-knowing, unchangeable. We have received life and being only because God has made us. We come to know God only as He reveals Himself to us in His words and in His works. Because Jesus speaks the words of God and does the works of God, we come to know Him as God.

From the Beginning

One of the most characteristic works of God can be seen in the story of creation. Before the creation God was alone. Solely through His will and His power, He brings forth something out of nothing. In creation God revealed Himself to be the living God, whose characteristic work is to give life. As the creation account makes clear, there can be no thought here of man assisting God in his creation. Man was just a lump of clay when God breathed into it and man became a living being (Genesis 2:7). Man's life is a pure gift, not something he has in himself. He has only received it. God, therefore, reveals Himself as the gracious God who gives and preserves life.

This is why John's Gospel begins the story of Jesus with the words "Through Him all things were made . . . in Him was life" (John 1:3–4). As the Word through whom God created the world ("And God said": Genesis 1:3, 6, 9, 11, 14), Jesus is the One who gives life. He renews the life of fallen and sinful mankind and is the One who has life in Himself. That is, Jesus is the living God. Jesus said, "I am the resurrection and the life" (John 11:25).

From this perspective, we come to recognize Jesus' miracles as demonstrations of His true divinity. Jesus reveals himself as true God through His commanding authority over nature and all created things. Therefore, when Jesus calms the sea (Luke 8:22–25), heals the paralyzed (Matthew 9:1–8), gives sight to the blind (Matthew 9:27–30), raises the dead (Matthew 9:18–25; John 11:5–44), He shows Himself to be the good Creator who creates out of nothing and who gives life to that which has no life. In all these ways, Jesus shows that He is God and desires that all have life and participate in the good gifts of God.

Jesus was also true man. He had flesh and bones, hair and blood. He had a human will and a human intellect. He was born of a woman. He experienced temptations and suffered anxiety, fear, and sorrow. He was under the Law of God. He was capable of suffering and death.

However, Jesus was not true man only because He was made of flesh and blood. He was true man in that He was a man just as God created man before the fall. He was without sin. Hence, Scripture often refers to Jesus as the new Adam. He was true man also in the sense that He was the perfectly sinless, obedient, and faithful son of God who served God in righteousness, innocence, and blessedness. Jesus was true man in that, despite temptation, fear, weakness, suffering, and death, He still believed God and did God's will, never doubting the gracious goodness of His heavenly Father as the good Creator. The Letter to the Hebrews speaks of Jesus as One who in every way shared in our flesh and blood, in our temptations, and in our sufferings and death:

> *Since the children have flesh and blood, He too shared in their humanity so that by His death He might destroy him who holds the power of death— that is, the devil—and free those who all their lives were held in slavery by their fear of death. . . . For this reason He had to be made like His brothers in every way, in order that He might become a merciful and faithful high priest in service to God, and that He might make atonement for the sins of the*

*people. Because He Himself suffered when He was
tempted, He is able to help those who are being
tempted. . . . For we do not have a high priest who is
unable to sympathize with our weaknesses, but we
have one who has been tempted in every way, just
as we are—yet was without sin. (Hebrews 2:14–18;
4:15)*

Created by the Creator

Jesus was like us in every way, but with one exception—He did not
sin. (See 1 Peter 2:22–24; 3:18.) We sometimes get the idea that Jesus
was sinless because He was God and hence could not sin. However, it is
important for us to understand what it means to be true man. We are
human. But because of the fall into sin and our own personal sin, we
are not what God intended us to be. Jesus is true man in that He is
exactly as God intended man to be, which includes His sinlessness. To
be truly human means to live as God's creature, as one who received
God's good gifts and perfectly trusts God as the gracious Creator who
will not withhold anything that is good and beneficial to mankind. To be
truly human means to live for God alone and to acknowledge God as
Lord and Giver of life. To be truly human is to let God be God for us.

Perhaps the creation story can also be helpful in this context. As we
noted, the creation revealed God as the gracious Creator who freely
and graciously gives life to man. However, as we also noted, man in no
way cooperated in his creation; Adam was a lump of clay when God
breathed into it. When Adam, the lump of clay, received God's inbreathing, Adam breathed. God's creative inbreathing became Adam's breathing. Had God withdrawn His breath from Adam, Adam would have
died. Adam's life is God's giving of life.

Now, it is no less Adam's breathing just because it results only from God's inbreathing. Yet the creation account helps us to understand that from the Bible's point of view, man is always seen as God's creature who receives life and every blessing from God, and from God alone. Conversely, man is never shown in the Bible to be a purely self-sufficient, independent being who can stand on his own.

Man is a creature, and that implies a Creator. But that is simply to say that man is always in relation to another, namely, to God. True man relates to God as one who thankfully and in trust receives from God. Sinful man relates to God also, but as one who rejects God and rebels against Him.

As the one who received his life and every blessing from God and who freely obeyed God's will, Adam was true man. As one who joyfully and freely lived from God's goodness, Adam was in the "image of God." He reflected what God had given to Him.

However, when Adam turned away from God and listened to Satan, Adam turned from the real source of all good things and sought his life from other things. Adam became an unbeliever, one who does not trust God as the good Giver of all things. In this unbelief, Adam became a sinner and inherited death (Romans 5:12).

Fallen Creation

Rejecting God as the source of every good blessing and seeking his well-being elsewhere, Adam ceased to be the creature who in thanks and trust received from God's hand. He became the sinner who seeks after his own good. Man became proud (thought himself independent from God) and selfish (sought his own good). Adam ceased to be "true man."

In a very important sense, therefore, when we sin, when we give way to the temptation of the devil, when we experience death, we are not truly human. We may be flesh and blood, but we do not trust God fully and readily with a thankful heart and an obedient will.

You have probably heard the old saying "To err is human." But from the point of view of the Bible, to err is *not* human. We are, of course, speaking here of sins and not merely making common mistakes. But this point is important: To be true man is to live as God created man to live, namely, as one who thankfully receives from the gracious hand of God.

Therefore, sinlessness does not simply mean not doing anything wrong. Sin is not just disobeying God's Law. Sin also involves not doing what we ought to do. And perhaps most important, sin refers to the posture of rebellion, pride, and assumed independence we have adopted toward God. Jesus was sinless, but not because He was God and could not sin. He was sinless because He was truly man. Jesus was the new Adam.

His sinlessness did not consist only in the fact that He did no wrong, but also in the fact that He trusted God at all times and in all circumstances. For that reason He freely obeyed God in an active and vigorous life of prayer, thanksgiving, self-sacrificing love, humility, patience, and long-suffering. The true humanity of Jesus is evident in all those activities in which He is the thankful and trusting recipient of God's good gifts.

We recognize Jesus' humanity in His birth, for there Jesus received life by the Holy Spirit through the Virgin Mary. We recognize His humanity in His eating and drinking, for in these He received God's gifts by which His human life is nurtured and preserved. We recognize His humanity in His sleeping, for in that He received a daily refreshment for the reinvigoration of earthly life.

But we recognize Jesus' true humanity also in His praying, in His giving thanks before meals, in His faith, in His works of love and forgiveness, and in His refusal to yield to the temptations of the devil. Note what Jesus says to Satan, who is tempting Jesus to worship him: "Worship the Lord your God, and serve Him only!" (Matthew 4:10). Such are the words of one who is true man.

Putting It All Together

Jesus is true God in that He is the Giver of life and of all good things. Jesus is true man in that He thankfully receives God's gifts and in perfect trust lives a sinless, obedient life. This is the divine design.

As true man Jesus is the image of our hope, for He is what we shall become. Jesus is the new Adam, the One in whom God has again made mankind according to His image, the One in whom God has again made true man, man who lives from God alone, trusts God alone, and serves God alone.

We used the story of creation to help us see true God at work and true man at work. We saw that through the living God's breathing life into Adam, Adam became himself a living being. In true man, God's work becomes man's work. God and man are in agreement; they are in communion with each other, united with each other. And so it is also in Jesus Christ, who is true God and true man. In the person of Jesus, God's work once again becomes man's work. Whereas once man cursed his neighbor, now the new Adam blesses his neighbor. Whereas once sinful man was selfish, now the new Adam gives charity freely and loves his neighbor as himself. Whereas sinful man once held grudges and got revenge, now the new Adam forgives his enemies.

The full Law of God, set in the heart of man at creation, now receives its complete and perfect fulfillment in Jesus. Christ did this for us who are sinners so that the penalty of sin, namely death, is not our final destiny, but that we might have eternal life in Him, who as the one great true man, and the new Adam, received life freely from God.

In Jesus, therefore, God renews this creation by making sinful man to become true man through the forgiveness of sins. In Jesus sinful man becomes true man, the image of God. Receiving his life from God, he "reflects" the holiness and righteousness of God in a holy and righteous life. (See 1 Peter 2:15–16; and especially Romans 8:1–4.)

One further point must be made clear. When the apostle John saw the new heaven and the new earth, he saw the community God's faithful people shall have with Him. This communion with God shall be forever and ever (Revelation 22:5). John's Gospel promises that whoever believes in Christ shall receive eternal life (John 3:15–16). Our redemption in Christ shall never come to an end. In Christ, God's good purposes for mankind will never be subject to temptation, decay, and death.

In Christ, God put His creation on a new and more solid foundation. In Christ, God united Himself with man in an inseparable and indivisible way, so that into all eternity man will be with God, receiving all good things, especially life and immortality.

Wherein does this new solidity and permanence for the future of man's communion with God lie? It lies in this: In Christ Jesus, God Himself became man. The eternal Word of God (the Second Person of the Trinity) took to Himself all that man is, and without ceasing to be true God made in Himself the start of a new creation wherein fallen, sinful, and mortal mankind becomes righteous, holy, and immortal. Since in Christ God has become man, in Christ man will be without sin and not be subject to eternal death. In Christ—the new Adam—man will never again act apart from God.

Our Savior

One concluding thought. Sometimes we think that because Jesus was God He did not really have to face what we face. The thought goes something like this: Because Jesus was God, He did not really fear death. Deep down He knew that since He was God, death could not hold Him. Or, because Jesus was God, He did not really feel the enticements of sin. He was not really tempted so that He could actually have fallen into sin, and therefore His temptations did not really challenge His very soul. Since Jesus was God He could not have sinned. Therefore His temptations were not serious temptations like those we face. Sometimes we all feel this way.

When we think such thoughts, it helps to remember that Jesus is our Savior. A savior is one who brings another out of a real danger. Jesus is Savior because although He was tempted in every way we are, He did not sin. Jesus is Savior because He went through temptation, yet continued to obey God and to trust in God. Jesus is Savior, not only because He is God and therefore above all our weaknesses, but also because having been in our weaknesses, having been tempted, having feared for His life, having agonized, having been rejected by family and friends, He did not stray from that singular and narrow path of His calling to be God's Son in whom God was well pleased. Finally, Jesus is our Savior because of His sacrificial death on the cross and His resurrection from the grave.

In Christ, therefore, we pass from sin to holiness, we pass from death to life.

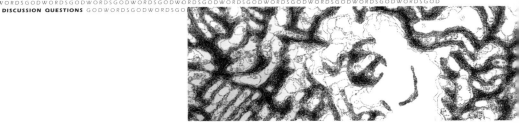

Discussion Questions

If you were to write your own confession of faith in Jesus, what kinds of things would you include?

What things about Jesus are especially important to you?

What does it mean when we say that Jesus was "true man"?

What does it mean that Jesus was "true God"?

Why does Jesus have to be both true man and true God if He is really the Messiah?

What does Jesus' sinlessness mean for Christians?

What does it mean to you that, in Christ, God takes sinful man and makes him true man?

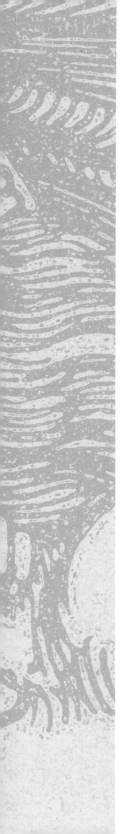

8

The Holy Spirit

BY WILLIAM WEINRICH

I believe in the Holy Spirit, the holy *Christian Church, the communion of saints, the forgiveness of sins, the resurrection of the body, and the life everlasting. (Third Article of the Apostles' Creed)*

How ordinary, even commonplace, the Apostles' Creed is in these words! To be sure, "the resurrection of the body" and "life everlasting" promise high excitement and give us great expectations. But forgiveness of sins?! Church?! The Nicene Creed also speaks of Baptism. These things seem so everyday, so common, so—dare we say it?—boring! You may not even remember when you were baptized, especially if you were baptized as a baby. The church may seem to be more an assembly of hypocrites than a gathering of saints. And the forgiveness of sins seems so simple, perhaps too simple.

Today we often hear of the Holy Spirit in terms quite different from those in the Apostles' Creed. The Holy Spirit is said to be a "power source" through which life becomes one victory after another. We hear of victorious living. In the Spirit, life is said to become extraordinary, special, a "high." We even hear about "special" gifts. Some people claim to have a "special" prayer language. Some say that they speak a "special" language of the Spirit, that they speak in tongues. Many say they have received a "special baptism" of the Spirit that has changed their lives, turned them around, and filled them with fullness of joy, peace, power, and self-confidence.

How incredibly certain and assured such persons may seem! How close to Jesus they appear! How filled with joy and abundant living! Sometimes they seem to have something we do not have. Their lives seem different.

Are individuals who do not have these "spiritual gifts" missing out on something great and wonderful? Are they quenching the Spirit? Perhaps a special baptism in the Spirit really is necessary to be a "real" Christian, to know Jesus personally as Lord and Savior. If the life of the Spirit is "new" life, doesn't it stand to reason that it should be marvelous, wonderful, exciting, and extraordinary?

But, what if one has doubts about God and feels that God is some-times far away? What if one doesn't speak in tongues or has never been overwhelmed by a baptism of the Spirit? Does such "silence" of the Spirit indicate a second-class Christianity, a kind of "doubting-Thomas Christianity," which places obstacles in the way of the free working of the Spirit? Does our "low-key" Christianity mean that we do not know Jesus as our personal Savior as we should?

These are important questions because they ask these questions: Who is a Christian? What is a Christian? How is a Christian a Christian?

It is clear that when we talk about the Holy Spirit, we are also talk-ing about the character of the Christian life. For this reason, Paul writes that the Christian lives "according to the Spirit" (Romans 8:4), that is, lives and acts according to the Spirit's working in him.

Proper Discernment

Let us do a little of what Paul calls "discerning" the Spirit and ask these questions: What is the work of the Holy Spirit? What does the Spirit's work "look" like?

Perhaps the best place to find an answer to such a question is to consider the one life that was fully under the Spirit's guidance, namely, the life of Jesus, the Son of God. All four Gospels say that from the beginning Jesus' life was guided and molded by the Holy Spirit. Luke tells us that from the conception of Jesus in Mary's womb the Spirit was active. Jesus was under the Spirit even before He was born (Luke 1:35).

All the Gospels tell of Jesus' baptism in the Jordan River, during which he received the Holy Spirit. The Gospels also make it clear that throughout the life and ministry of Jesus the Holy Spirit was active. According to John, the Holy Spirit remained on Jesus (John 1:32). Luke tells us that Jesus was "led by the Spirit in the desert, where for forty days He was tempted by the devil" and that Jesus returned to Galilee after the temptation "in the power of the Spirit" (Luke 4:1–2, 4). All of Jesus' life, therefore, shows forth the work of the Spirit. We can also turn this statement around and say that the work of the Spirit always takes the "shape" of Jesus' life.

But what was the "shape" of Jesus' life? What was so special about His life that shows it to be life according to the Spirit?

First, it might be helpful to say what did not make it special. Jesus did miracles; nowhere do the Gospels tell us that Jesus spoke in tongues or that He had revelations and visions. Nowhere does it say that He experienced ecstasies or that He had a special baptism of the Spirit that many Christians feel you must have. It was not these kinds of things that made Jesus' life a life according to the Spirit.

Yet Jesus was the true Son of God, full of grace and truth. He had complete and perfect unity with the Father. He is the way and the truth and the life (John 14:6).

If Jesus did not receive "special" gifts (or if they're not important enough to be reported in the Bible), they obviously cannot be said to be necessary signs of the power and presence of the Spirit. This does not necessarily mean that such gifts do not exist or that such gifts are not given and received in our own time. But they are not necessary for salvation or for a full and complete Christian life. They are gifts we can do without. If "special" gifts are not central to the life of Christ, "special" gifts should not be central to the Christian life.

Okay, then, what was the "shape" of Jesus' life that shows it to have been of the Spirit? Jesus Himself summarized His life and its purpose:

"The Son of Man did not come to be served, but to serve, and to give His life as a ransom for many" (Matthew 20:28). The suffering and death of Jesus, giving of the gift of Himself, is the "shape" of Jesus' life. All that He said and did bore the imprint of the cross.

When Jesus ate with sinners and tax collectors (Matthew 9:10–11), He was not just being friendly. Jesus was showing forth His cross, extending His love to those who were without love and embracing the outcast and the sinner with His presence. When Jesus spoke words of forgiveness (Matthew 9:2), He was showing forth His cross, for His death was for the forgiveness of sins (John 1:29). It is important that we not think of Jesus' death on the cross simply as the last thing Jesus did. Rather, Jesus' death on the cross was like a prism that caught the light of God's love and scattered that light into the multitude of individual works and words that Jesus did. Everything that Jesus did and said reflected the light of the cross.

The "shape" of Jesus' life was that of the cross. The cross-shaped life of Jesus is not just a life lived a long time ago, like that of George Washington or Julius Caesar. Washington and Caesar died a long time ago, and although they were important figures in history, they do not now have a direct and personal relationship with us. They do not influence us, direct us, or rule us.

This is not the case with Jesus. Jesus is raised from the dead and now lives. And there is more! Jesus lives in such a way that He now guides us, directs us, teaches us, loves us, and is our Master. That is all to say, Jesus is Lord! But according to the apostle Paul, it is through the Holy Spirit that we confess, "Jesus is Lord" (1 Corinthians 12:3).

Here is the key to understanding the work of the Holy Spirit. He enables us to believe in Christ and confess Him as Lord.

What's in a Name?

What does it mean to be Lord? It does not mean merely to have power and authority. To be Lord is not just to be the strongest. Rather, to be Lord means to exercise rule or to exert influence so that others conform to the image of the person who is Lord.

Most of us have favorite music performers. They may have a distinctive look—hair, makeup, clothes, and jewelry work together to portray their look. The more popular a star is, the more probable their fans show their loyalty by adopting that look as their own. They show themselves to be fans by imitating the rock star. In a way, therefore, the star is "lord" of his/her fans, and the fans recognize the star as their "lord" by conforming to his/her image.

It is no different with Jesus. When we confess, "Jesus is Lord," we are not merely saying we believe that Jesus is God or that Jesus is in heaven. We are not only saying something about Jesus. We are rather speaking of Jesus as the One to whom we are loyal—the One whom we wish to imitate—the One after whose image we wish to pattern ourselves. Using the image of "shape" once more, if Jesus is our Lord, we will adopt the "shape" of Jesus' life for our own life.

The "disciples" of a music star imitate him/her even though they do not personally know the star and are not personally known by him/her. The imitation of a star, therefore, is like the imitation of a parrot: what it sees or hears in another it chooses for itself. But that is not the way it is with Jesus. He, as our Creator and Savior, knows us and gives Himself to us as a free gift.

What does it mean that Jesus gives Himself to us? It means He makes Himself our Lord. When Jesus gives Himself to us, we come to know Him as our Savior, we receive Him as our Lord. We are conformed to His image and receive the "shape" of His life.

Remember the apostle Paul's words: "No one can say, 'Jesus is Lord,' except by the Holy Spirit" (1 Corinthians 12:3). It is the Holy Spirit who brings Jesus to us and causes us to recognize Jesus as our Lord. We receive His image and the "shape" of His life. Those to whom the Spirit comes receive Jesus as Lord and are patterned after Him.

The apostle Paul writes of this in the following way: "And we, who with unveiled faces all reflect the Lord's glory, are being transformed into His likeness with ever-increasing glory, which comes from the Lord, who is the Spirit" (2 Corinthians 3:18). Simply stated, the work of the Holy Spirit is to bring us to faith and to turn us into the image of Christ, to shape our thoughts and our lives so that we reflect Jesus, who is the Lord.

How does the Holy Spirit accomplish this work of making Jesus our Lord, of giving us Jesus as our Savior, of conforming us to the "shape" of Jesus' life? This is a very important question. The answer to this question explains why the Third Article of the Creed concerning the Holy Spirit also mentions the church, Baptism, the forgiveness of sins, and the resurrection of the body.

We all are familiar with political campaigns and elections. What happens in a campaign? The candidates running for office speak of their past accomplishments and argue for their ideas and opinions. The idea is that these accomplishments and opinions are so good and desirable that the voters will want such actions and views to continue into the future. If a candidate's record of what he has done and thought in the past were no guide whatsoever for what we could expect of him in the future, we would surely not vote for such an unclear, uncertain, and unpredictable candidate. We would rather vote for a candidate whose past record indicates what the candidate will continue to do in the future.

Using the example of the candidate, we may think of Jesus as the candidate put forward and elected by God the Father to continue His words and His work. If we ask when or how did the Father "elect" Jesus to continue His words and work, the answer is when the Father raised Jesus from the dead and exalted Jesus, that is, made Him to be Lord of all. The apostle Paul speaks of this in Philippians 2:9–11: "Therefore God exalted Him to the highest place and gave Him the name that is above every name, that at the name of Jesus every knee should bow, in heaven and on earth and under the earth, and every tongue confess that Jesus Christ is Lord, to the glory of God the Father."

By raising Jesus from the dead and making Him to be Lord over all, the Father ensured that the ministry of service of Jesus would continue. But after His resurrection the Lord Jesus would work through His disciples, who in the power of the Holy Spirit would speak the words of Jesus and do His deeds.

It is significant that the Gospels conclude their story of Jesus' life with the sending of the disciples and that this sending is connected with the coming of the Holy Spirit. The Gospel of Matthew ends its account with the commissioning of the disciples: "Go and make disciples of all nations . . . teaching them to obey everything I have commanded you" (Matthew 28:19–20). In the Gospel of Luke this commissioning is connected with the gift of the Holy Spirit. By the power of the Holy Spirit, the disciples preach repentance and the forgiveness of sins to all nations (Luke 24:47). Similarly, at the end of the Gospel of John, Jesus explicitly compares the Father sending Him with His sending of the disciples: "As the Father has sent Me, I am sending you" (John 20:21). Then Jesus says, "Receive the Holy Spirit. If you forgive anyone his sins, they are forgiven; if you do not forgive them, they are not forgiven" (John 20:22–23).

The Gospels end with the sending of the disciples and the gift of the Holy Spirit because they want us to know that the story of Jesus is not over. Having been raised from the dead, Jesus lives, and by His ascension into heaven Jesus lives as Lord. That is, Jesus lives as the One who rules us, guides us, and continues to forgive our sins. And all this Jesus does through the power of the Holy Spirit.

If we keep this in mind, the story of the coming of the Holy Spirit at Pentecost in Acts 2 becomes easily understandable. You know the story. The disciples are gathered together when all of a sudden there is the sound of rushing wind. Tongues of fire appear on their heads, and the disciples begin to speak in the languages of many nations (Acts 2:1–12). What is important about this story is not so much the incidentals, such as the rushing wind and the tongues of fire, but rather its place in the whole story of Acts.

The Book of Acts begins with the story of the ascension of Jesus into heaven. The fact that the story of Jesus' ascension comes first is important. It means that everything Acts tells of afterward is, in fact, the work of the Lord Jesus Himself. The ascension of Jesus, therefore, does not mean that Jesus went away to another place, distant and apart from us. Indeed, Jesus promised that He would be with us to the end of the age (Matthew 28:20). Rather, the ascension of Jesus is the event by which Jesus became Lord so that He can continue to be present as He was present in His earthly ministry.

The story of Pentecost tells us that through the Holy Spirit Jesus rules as the heavenly King. For this reason the story of Pentecost comes after the story of Jesus' ascension. The heavenly lordship of Jesus happens through the working of the Holy Spirit.

And—this is very important—the work of Jesus through the Holy Spirit happens in the sending of the disciples into the world to preach about Jesus, to baptize, to forgive sins. That is why when the Holy Spirit comes upon the disciples at Pentecost, Peter immediately begins to preach about Jesus, His death and resurrection, and this preaching leads the hearers straightway to repentance and Baptism for the forgiveness of sins (Acts 2:1–38). Through the preaching of forgiveness by the disciples, Jesus continues to forgive sins. The preaching of the disciples is through the power of the Holy Spirit, for Jesus continues His work through the Spirit.

The Bible often connects witnessing to Jesus with the Holy Spirit. According to Mark, those who witness about Jesus during times of persecution are speaking by the Holy Spirit (Mark 13:11). John's Gospel simply says that the Spirit "testifies" concerning Jesus (John 15:26). The Spirit will teach what Jesus has taught and will cause the disciples of Jesus to remember Jesus' words (John 14:26). All of this is to say that Jesus is present as the One who forgives in the preaching of forgiveness through Jesus' death and resurrection.

The Spirit Reveals Christ

What, then, is the work of the Holy Spirit? The Holy Spirit brings Jesus and His work of forgiveness to us now, here in our own lives. Where does the Holy Spirit do this? Wherever the forgiveness of sins through Jesus' death and resurrection is proclaimed. Let us mention the most important occasions when our sins are forgiven: (1) through the preaching of our pastors, whose sermons proclaim Jesus as the crucified Savior; (2) in absolution, when the pastor forgives our sins after we have confessed them; (3) in Baptism, which the apostle Paul says is being buried with Christ and rising with Him; and (4) in the Lord's Supper, during which we eat Christ's body, given for the forgiveness of sins, and drink His blood, shed for the sins of all.

Earlier we asked, "What does the Spirit's work "look like"? We can now answer—the Spirit's work "looks" like the cross; it has the "shape" of the cross. The Spirit is at work wherever and whenever the death and resurrection of Jesus is preached and proclaimed. The Spirit works through preaching, through missions, through evangelism, through Baptism, through the Lord's Supper. The Spirit works in all of these things, for in them Jesus works as He once worked on earth. As He once forgave the paralytic, so now He forgives us. This is the work of the Holy Spirit.

Can we then be saved without the Holy Spirit? No, for only through the Spirit, that is, only through the Word and the Sacraments, do we receive Jesus as our Lord and Savior. In the Large Catechism, Martin Luther writes in the same way: "For where Christ is not preached, there is no Holy Spirit to create, call, and gather the Christian church, and outside it no one can come to the Lord Christ" (Large Catechism II 45).

Jesus is not only our Savior, but also our Lord. He is our Lord because in His death and resurrection He defeated the devil, ascended into heaven, and now rules and fills all things. Jesus comes as Lord to us through the Holy Spirit, by whose power Jesus' death and resurrection are proclaimed (preached) and given (Sacraments).

Jesus becomes our Lord when we receive Him and make Him our own. This, therefore, is also the work of the Holy Spirit, that we receive Jesus as our Lord. This receiving of Jesus as our Lord is called faith, and for this reason we say that one must have faith to be saved. To have faith is to know Jesus as Savior from sin and Lord of our lives. The Holy Spirit gives us faith.

Discipleship

Remember what we said about the meaning of the confession "Jesus is Lord"? It means that we are conformed to the image of Jesus, who is our Lord. It is finally also the work of the Holy Spirit that we are conformed to Jesus, that is, receive the shape of Jesus' life as the shape of our own lives. And that shape is the cross.

Jesus spoke of discipleship as taking up his cross and following Him (Luke 9:23). Paul speaks of discipleship as "crucify[ing] the sinful nature with its passions and desires" (Galatians 5:24; note the "cross" language Paul uses). And now we can understand why the Bible speaks of the "fruit" of the Spirit as "love, joy, peace, patience, kindness, goodness, faithfulness, gentleness and self-control" (Galatians 5:22–23). Such virtues were characteristic of Jesus' life. He loved. He was long-suffering. He was faithful. He was gentle. When the Spirit conforms us to the image of Jesus—to His cross-shaped life—such virtues characterize our lives as well. Such behavior is not a sign of weakness or timidity, but rather is rooted in the power of God, who through Jesus' cross defeated sin and the devil.

People frequently speak of the Holy Spirit as some sort of special "power source" for victorious living. Hopefully, we have come to see that God's power and God's victory are in the cross of Jesus our Lord and that, therefore, our power and our victory are also in the cross of Jesus. We have this power and victory of God in Jesus through the Holy Spirit. Just as the power and victory of God was revealed in the suffering of the Savior, so also our power and victory in the cross is demonstrated in the lowliness of simple faith and a Christian life. Therefore when we doubt God's goodness or when we wonder why we continue to sin and do wrong or have thoughts we would rather not think, the work of the Spirit will cause you to remember that in His death and resurrection Jesus is Lord also for us. In Him there is forgiveness and power for living.

Discussion Questions

*What would you say to a friend who says a
Christian should speak in tongues to prove his faith
and the Holy Spirit's activity in his life?*

*Did Jesus possess the so-called "special gifts"?
Why is this a significant question?*

*What is the function of the Holy Spirit?
What does He do? What means does He use?*

*What do you understand the concept of "the shape
of life is the shape of the cross" to mean? What did it
mean to Jesus? What does it mean for you?*

*Why do the Gospels end with the sending of the
disciples and the gift of the Holy Spirit?*

9

The Means of Grace

BY PAUL RAABE

Linda was depressed. The previous day she had done some things she knew were wrong and sinful. She felt very guilty. Her conscience bothered her. In church she often heard about Judgment Day. Now she was afraid that God might condemn her for her sins. What should Linda do?

Richard visited his grandfather, who was dying of cancer, in the hospital. His grandfather kept wondering why God let this happen. He concluded that God hated him and was punishing him for his sins. Richard could tell that his grandfather was very fearful of death and the prospect of facing God. What should Richard say?

What advice would you give Linda and Richard? People might offer all kinds of advice. Some would say that despairing persons should look deep inside themselves and feel God's love. But feelings are fickle; sometimes you feel good and sometimes you don't. Others might advise the despairing to pray earnestly and surrender themselves totally to God. But you never know if you have prayed earnestly enough or completely surrendered yourself to God.

Some might advise that one should simply think positively and get rid of all negative feelings. But that is pretty hard to do when you are afraid of God and what He might do to you. Still others would advise communing with God in nature. But the god found in nature is ambiguous too. On a nice day the god in nature appears to be kind and loving. But when the weather is stormy and threatening, nature's god may appear to be mean, angry, and hateful.

People who are hurting need a gracious and kind God, a God who loves them and cares about them. The hurting person needs Jesus Christ. At the cross of Christ one finds the gracious God. But where does one find Christ and His cross?

This is where the biblical teaching of the means of grace comes in. A Lutheran Christian who believes, teaches, and confesses what the Scriptures teach would direct Linda and the dying grandfather and any hurting friend not to themselves but outside of themselves, to the means of grace through which they receive the forgiveness of sins and God's favor on account of Christ.

The means of grace is a term that refers to the vehicles, the channels, the instruments, the "means" through which God offers and conveys His mercy to people. In the means of grace God's people receive the forgiveness of sin, life, and salvation which Christ earned by His life, death, and resurrection. The means of grace are the vehicles through which the Holy Spirit creates and sustains faith.

The means of grace are the places where Christ is graciously present for you. Christ is everywhere, but we are not. We live in a certain place at a certain time. So Christ graciously relates to sinful people by making His merciful presence and gifts available to them in certain external places. He has located them in the means of grace—the Gospel, Baptism, and the Lord's Supper.

There has always been a "locatedness" to God's gracious presence and gifts. In the Old Testament the faithful in Israel longed to go to the tabernacle and later to the temple on Mount Zion (Deuteronomy 16:16; Psalm 84:10; Psalm 122).

Why were the tabernacle and temple so significant? Because God graciously dwelt among His people there. Here God was graciously present for His people. Here He put His saving name (Exodus 29:42–46; 40:34–38; Deuteronomy 14:23; Psalm 48). They were the places where

Israel would receive God's blessings (Exodus 20:24; Deuteronomy 10:8; Psalm 132:13–16). At the tabernacle and temple, the omnipresent God was present for Israel. He, by grace, forgave the repentant sinners, declared them just, and reconciled them to Himself. God conveyed these gifts through the Word of the Gospel spoken by the priest (Numbers 6:22–27; Deuteronomy 10:8) and through the sacrifices (Leviticus 1:3–4; 16:30; 17:11). The Gospel and the sacrifices were Old Testament means of grace. Through these means Christ conveyed to His "B.C." people the benefits of His all-sufficient, atoning, sacrificial death and resurrection.

The New Testament also teaches that Christ is graciously present with His gifts in certain external places, in the Gospel and the Sacraments. So when we want to receive and be comforted by the gifts Christ gives, we go to the means of grace.

Don't go to nature; don't look inside yourself for inner strength; don't simply try harder or pray more or think positively. Go to the vehicles through which God gives His gifts.

The Means of Grace and the Church

The means of grace are called the "marks" of the church since through them God grants forgiveness, life, and salvation. They are the means Christ uses to found and preserve His church. Where these means are dispensed, you can be sure that Christ's "holy, catholic, and apostolic church" is there. They identify where the assembly of believers is to be found. Therefore, it is always important for a Christian congregation to preserve and teach the pure Gospel, administer the Sacraments in accordance with God's Word, and to resist false teaching, which pulls people away from Christ's Word and Sacraments.

Dispensing the means of grace is the way in which the church "make[s] disciples of all nations" (Matthew 28:19), since the Holy Spirit is at work through them. God wants us to proclaim and console despairing sinners with the Gospel. We are called to encourage them to be baptized if they are not (Acts 2:38), or, if they have been baptized, to remind them what God did through it (Romans 6). We are to encourage our fellow church members to receive the Lord's Supper often and to remind each other of what Christ gives through it. The means of grace are the marks of the church and the church's greatest treasures. We should always thank God for these great gifts.

Gospel

By Christ's death and resurrection, God reconciled (put into friendship with Himself) all people unto Himself. His wrath was appeased, and He forgave them. Gospel means "Good News." It is the "message of reconciliation" (2 Corinthians 5:19), the Good News that God has declared all sinners just by His grace on account of Christ (Romans 3:21–26).

The Gospel is not just a static message of words. Rather it is the message through which God works on people. The Gospel is "the power of God for the salvation" (Romans 1:16). It is the means through which the Holy Spirit creates and sustains saving faith (Romans 10:17). The Gospel is a means of grace in every form in which it reaches people, whether it be proclaimed (Luke 24:27; Galatians 3:2), printed (John 20:31; 1 John 1:3–4), expressed as formal absolution by the pastor "in the stead and by the command of my Lord Jesus Christ," pondered in the heart (Romans 10:8), or pictured in symbols (such as a crucifix) that lead one to remember Christ's work.

Where the Gospel is, there is Christ giving His gifts to the person who receives them by faith.

Therefore, it is important for you to read and hear regularly the

Gospel, through which the Holy Spirit strengthens your faith. And it is important for you to tell others about "Jesus Christ and Him crucified" (1 Corinthians 2:2) so that the Holy Spirit will work on them too.

Baptism

The Baptism of a little baby looks like such a humble, ordinary rite. People often wonder if anything significant happens, or if it is just a meaningless church ritual. What was the meaning of your own Baptism? Does it have any practical significance for your Christian life?

Its Institution and Essence

The Scriptures teach that Baptism was instituted and commanded by Christ (Matthew 28:19). It is the application of water in the name of the triune God (Ephesians 5:26; Matthew 28:19). Some churches insist that the application of water must be by immersion, but the Greek word *baptize* can also be translated "pouring water" (as in Luke 11:38; Mark 7:4). Therefore, the water can be applied by pouring, sprinkling, or immersing. But it is not just water. It is water connected with God's Word (Ephesians 5:26). It is applied in the name of the Father, Son, and Holy Spirit. We can call it a "visible Word," the Gospel connected with the water.

Many churches teach that Baptism is something that man does to confess faith, or which the congregation does to dedicate one to Christ. But the Scriptures teach that God is the One who acts on the recipient through Baptism. Baptism is God's work. Ephesians 5:26 says that Christ is "cleansing her [the church] through by the washing with water through the word." Titus 3:5 says that "[God] saved us . . . through the washing of rebirth and renewal by the Holy Spirit." Romans 6:4 states that "we were therefore buried with Him [Christ] through baptism into death."

These verses clearly teach that the triune God is the One who is acting in Baptism. He performs His saving act on the recipient through the means of water and Word. It is not simply a human decision or action. If it were, then it would be no big deal. But it is God's action and, therefore, it *is* a big deal.

Its Benefits

What does God do through Baptism? We can summarize the answer in three parts.

* *Christ assigns and incorporates the recipient into His atoning death and resurrection. When Christ died, the baptized person died with Him; when Christ was buried, the baptized person was buried with Him; when Christ was raised, the baptized person was raised with Him (Colossians 2:12; Romans 6:3–10). Before Baptism we were connected to Adam and thus dead in our sins and under the curse of death (Romans 5:12–21; 1 Corinthians 15:22). But through Baptism Christ has connected us to Himself and to His death and resurrection. Therefore, we have been forgiven (Colossians 2:13; Acts 2:38; 22:16), cleansed (Ephesians 5:26), declared just (1 Corinthians 6:11; Titus 3:5–7), born again (John 3:3–5), made dead to sin and alive to God (Romans 6:6–11), made sons of God and heirs of eternal life (Galatians 3:26–29), and guaranteed our future resurrection (Romans 6:5).*

* *Through Baptism God gave and "poured out on us generously" the Holy Spirit, who creates and sustains faith (Titus 3:3–6).*

* *Through Baptism Christ makes us members of His church, the assembly of believers (1 Corinthians 12:12–13). Just as circumcision made a newborn Israelite male a member of God's people (Genesis 17:9–14), so Baptism is the new, Christian circumcision (Colossians*

2:11–12). We are a part of the covenant community of God with His people.

Baptism has a very practical significance for your Christian life. Because your old Adam was crucified with Christ and you put on Christ through Baptism, you are daily to drown your old Adam and rise up to newness of life (Romans 6:1–14). You are to "set your mind on things above" (Colossians 3:2). In other words, your Baptism calls you to "be what you are," to live like a baptized child of God (Colossians 3:5–4:6).

Infant Baptism

Sometimes people wonder why Lutherans baptize babies. Many churches don't do this. There are four important points to keep in mind. First, Christ commands the church to baptize "all nations" (Matthew 28:19). Second, babies are "in Adam": they are sinners who need forgiveness and salvation just like everybody else. Third, Baptism is a means of grace through which God bestows Christ's salvation on the sinner. Fourth, through Baptism God gives His Holy Spirit, who creates saving faith in Christ. We baptize infants, confident that God will do what He promises.

The Lord's Supper

Christians who believe in Christ, believe, teach, and confess what His Word says about His Supper. In this section we will summarize what the Scriptures say. The key sections are Matthew 26:26–29; Mark 14:22–25; Luke 22:15–20; 1 Corinthians 10:14–22; and 1 Corinthians 11:17–34.

Its Institution

The Lord's Supper was instituted by Jesus "on the night He was betrayed" (1 Corinthians 11:23). Because He commanded, "Do this in remembrance of Me" (verse 24), the church of all ages is to celebrate it. (Compare Acts 2:42 and 1 Corinthians 11:23.)

It is important to notice the setting in which Christ instituted His Supper. He selected the night of the Passover meal (Matthew 26:17–19; Mark 14:12–16; Luke 22:7–15). The Passover festival commemorated how God spared His people from the angel of death and delivered them from Egyptian bondage (Exodus 12). This Old Testament event pointed to the deliverance won by Christ, the Lamb of God (1 Corinthians 5:7). This setting for the institution of the Lord's Supper was very appropriate. In His Supper Christ gives us His body and blood, which He sacrificed to deliver us from bondage to sin and death.

The Essence

The essence of the Lord's Supper is expressed in Jesus' words "Take and eat; this is My body. Drink from it, all of you. This is My blood" (Matthew 26:26–27). The elements Jesus used were bread and wine ("fruit of the vine," Matthew 26:29). Christ clearly says that His body and blood are truly present and distributed to eat and drink. St. Paul makes the same point: The cup is "a participation [or communion] in the blood of Christ" and the bread is "a participation [or communion] in the body of Christ" (1 Corinthians 10:16). Whoever, therefore, "eats the bread or drinks the cup of the Lord in an unworthy manner will be guilty of sinning against the *body* and *blood* of the Lord" (1 Corinthians 11:27, emphasis added). Lutherans confess this scriptural teaching by affirming that the body and blood of the crucified and risen Christ are *in, with,* and *under* the bread and wine. By this we are affirming Christ's clear words even though we cannot rationally understand *how* this is so.

Its Benefits

* *In His Supper Christ gives us all the blessings and benefits of His sacrificial death. Jesus says that His body is "given for you" (Luke 22:19), that His blood is "poured out for many" (Matthew 26:28; Mark 14:24). He stresses His sacrifice on the cross. With His body and blood sacrificed for us, He gives us the benefits of His sacrifice, "the forgiveness of sins" (Matthew 26:28). And where there is forgiveness of sin, there is life and salvation.*

* *By giving His body and His blood, Jesus renews His covenant, or promise, with us ("My blood of the covenant," Matthew 26:28; Mark 14:24; the "new covenant in My blood," Luke 22:20; 1 Corinthians 11:25). In the Old Testament God established His covenant with His people (Exodus 24:8). "I will take you as My own people, and I will be your God" (Exodus 6:7). In Jeremiah 31:31–34 He promises a "new covenant." Christ's death established this "new covenant" (Hebrews 8–9). Through the Lord's Supper Christ gives us the blessings of this new covenant: He forgives us and makes us His people.*

* *Through the Lord's Supper Christ gives us a foretaste of the messianic banquet He will have with His church when He returns in glory. As He says, "I tell you, I will not drink of this fruit of the vine from now on until that day when I drink it anew with you in My Father's kingdom" (Matthew 26:29; cf. Mark 14:25; Luke 22:16, 18; Revelation 19:7–9). At His Table we not only look to His First Advent, but also to His Second. When we receive the body and blood of our crucified and risen Lord, we receive a guarantee that we will rise and live with Him on the Last Day.*

In Holy Communion Christ strengthens the oneness we have with each other in His church. "Because there is one loaf, we, who are many, are one body, for we all partake of the one loaf" (1 Corinthians 10:17). His body, which we are given, "bodies" us together with each other. Communion is not just a matter between you and Christ, but also a matter between you and the others in the congregation.

Close Communion

Why do our congregations not allow all people to commune at their altars? Are we acting "snobbish" or "holier than thou"? Should you commune at a Presbyterian, Baptist, Catholic, or some other denomination's altar? Sometimes people wonder about these questions.

Those who believe, teach, and confess what the Lord says in the Bible about His Supper, desire to honor and obey His Word by reserving the Sacrament for those for whom Christ gives it. After all, it is the "Lord's Supper" (1 Corinthians 11:20), not our supper that we can alter and change to suit our fancy. In striving to be faithful to the scriptural teaching, we practice "close" Communion. It is Communion among those who are "close" to each other in their confession of faith; that is, we believe the same things about God and His grace through Jesus Christ.

The Scripture teaches that the Lord's Supper is to be given to the following:

1. Baptized Christians. Through Baptism Christ makes us members of His church (1 Corinthians 12:13); through the Lord's Supper He strengthens and nourishes a Christian's faith (1 Corinthians 11:17–22).

2. Those who are able to examine themselves (1 Corinthians 11:28), that is, those who repent and see their need for the Sacrament. Those who persist in open, willful sin and refuse to repent are excluded (1 Corinthians 5:11–13; 10:21).

3. Those who believe the words of our Lord that they receive the true body and blood of the Lord for the forgiveness of sin in the Sacrament. Jesus' Words of Institution call for faith in those words. St. Paul states that those who receive it without faith in the Words of Institution (unworthily, without discerning the Lord's body, 1 Corinthians 11:27, 29) are endangering their souls. They are eating and drinking judgment upon themselves (1 Corinthians 11:29). This provision excludes those of the Reformed churches, which deny that one eats and drinks Christ's body and blood in, with, and under the bread and wine. Reformed churches deny what the Lord means in His words and it is not certain whether they even have the Lord's Supper. The Lord's Supper is more a rite or ceremony and not a Sacrament through which God gives forgiveness to the partaker. Therefore, Lutherans should not attend Communion in Reformed churches.

4. Those who confess the true scriptural faith. The Lord unites us with Himself and therefore with each other in the Sacrament (1 Corinthians 10:16–17). We dare not thwart what He is trying to do at the Lord's Table by tolerating and condoning those who persist in false teaching and false confessions of faith. There is only "one Lord" and "one faith," and we are "eager to maintain the unity of the Spirit" (Ephesians 4:3–6). The Lord wants to keep us united in the one faith at the altar. We dare not allow disunity and factions to develop in our midst (1 Corinthians 11:18–19; 1:10). Nor should we go to Communion in heterodox churches, since we are not one in confession with them.

This is why our congregations do not practice open Communion—not due to snobbishness, but to the desire to be faithful to the Lord and out of love for people lest they take the Lord's Supper to their damnation.

Its Practical Significance

The Lord gave us a great treasure in His Supper. Through it He gives us His gifts and promises to strengthen our faith. Therefore, we will want to receive it often. We will receive it "in remembrance of" Christ and with faith in the words "given and shed for you." And we receive it with thanksgiving and joy. Sometimes it is called the "Eucharist" after the Greek word for giving thanks (Matthew 26:27; Mark 14:23; Luke 22:19; 1 Corinthians 11:24) to express this thankful joy.

Christians who receive the Lord's Supper in faith will, with the Lord's help, amend their lives using the gifts He gives. We will be reconciled with each other since we are one at the altar.

The means of grace are a great gift and treasure that the Lord has given His church. May we always thank and praise God for His gifts and faithfully make use of them.

Discussion Questions

What are the means of grace? What do they do?

Why are the means of grace called the marks of the church?

What is Baptism?

Why do Lutherans baptize babies?

What happens when you receive the Lord's Supper?

How often do you think you should take Communion? Why?

What does "close Communion" mean to you?

What's the difference between "close" and "closed"?

Why is close Communion a good practice for God's people?

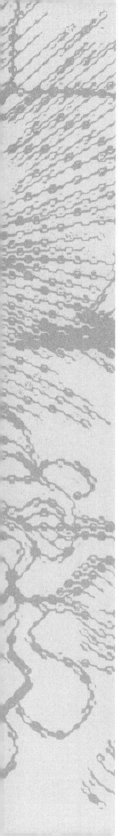

10

The Church of Jesus Christ

BY DAVID LUMPP

GODWORDSGODWORDSGODWORDSGODWORDSGODWORDSGODWORDSGODWORDSGODWORDSGODWORDSGODWORE
WORDSGODWORDSGODWORDSGODWORDSGODWORDSGODWORDSGODWORDSGODWORDSGODWORDSGODWORDSGO
GODWORDSGODWORDSGODWORDSGODWORDSGODWORDSGODWORDSGODWORDSGODWORDSGODWORDSGODWORE

"I believe in the Holy Spirit, the holy Christian church, the communion of saints." With these words the Apostles' Creed express-es the conviction that the church is the gathering, or community, of those whom the Holy Spirit has brought to faith in Jesus as their Savior from sin. In fact, the writers of the Creed recognized that one could not speak of either the church or the Holy Spirit in isolation from the other. The church owes its very existence to the Holy Spirit. By calling people to saving faith, He is in the process of building up the church.

In the New Testament the term frequently used to designate the church is *ekklesia* (pronounced ek-lay-see-a). It is the Greek term from which we derive "ecclesiastical," an adjective that means something like "related to the church." The Greek noun is a compound of two words (a preposition and a verb) and literally means "the called-out." The impor-tant point is that it represents Christians who have been separated from the surrounding world by their faith and their commitment to a life of discipleship. The New Testament concept of "call" here refers to God's action through Jesus Christ, by which He invites and draws people into a relation with Himself. (See 2 Timothy 1:9; Ephesians 1:18; 4:1.)

Above all, the calling action of God that brings people into the church is "through Jesus Christ." This phrase summarizes the entire action of God. First, the emphasis is on the "Gospel action" in which the Father sends His Son to redeem sinful humanity through His own suffer-ing and death (Colossians 1:12–20). Also absolutely crucial is God's raising Jesus from the dead. If that were not enough, God "packages" this message and commissions the Word of the Gospel. In Jesus Christ our sins have been forgiven unconditionally, and we are free to serve God without the constant fear that our standing before Him depends on the quantity or quality of the things we do.

The Gospel has a transforming effect on people. It makes disciples out of people who were formerly hostile or indifferent toward God. Using the verb "to call," the apostle Peter describes what takes place with the aid of popular Old Testament terminology:

> *But you are a chosen people, a royal priesthood, a*
> *holy nation, a people belonging to God, that you*
> *may declare the praises of Him who called you out*
> *of darkness into His wonderful light. Once you were*
> *not a people, but now you are the people of God;*
> *once you had not received mercy, but now you have*
> *received mercy. (1 Peter 2:9–10)*

Here we have introduced another central feature of God's calling action. The Gospel that brings us into the church is a continuing call, one that does not stop with us. It is an abiding summons and invitation, with no long list of spiritual prerequisites.

Can one be a Christian without being a part of this church? Can one just read his or her Bible and have fellowship with Jesus in that way?

These are not really the questions we should ask. In the first place, everyone who has saving faith in Jesus is, through that very faith, a member of the holy Christian church. Regarding the second question, one does have fellowship with Jesus through the spiritual nourishment His Word brings. But that's not really the point either.

Why would anyone choose to remain apart from the rest of the family of God, and in so doing cut oneself off from the sacramental life of the church? Also, how can anyone pursue a life of discipleship in spiritual isolation from the fellowship of the church? We all need to hear the word of pardon God speaks to us in the worship service of the congregation. Throughout the New Testament we see that local churches arose wherever the apostle preached. God intends that His children have contact with one another and use the means of grace together. (See especially Hebrews 10:25.)

To state matters simply, the significance of the church (and of our role in it) is to be the agency, setting, and vehicle through which God's call in Christ—His Gospel Word of grace and forgiveness—keeps coming to His people (Ephesians 4:1–16).

Perhaps you have come to know or experience the church primarily through your local congregation. You may be familiar with its structure, organization, or leadership. It is important to note, however, that as useful as such things are, they are not themselves the essence of the church. In Lutheran theology, the essence of the church is consistently defined in terms of *people*, specifically, those people who trust in Jesus Christ as their Savior. The church is an assembly of Christian people gathered in the name of Jesus. This takes us back again to the Third Article of the Apostles' Creed, with which we began. Here "communion of saints" is an explanation or amplification of the term "church." The church is the gathering of believing people.

Listen to Martin Luther's "people-oriented" definition of the church. This might well be the most popular definition of the church in the entire Lutheran theological tradition: "Thank God, a seven-year-old child knows what the church is, namely, holy believers and sheep who hear the voice of their Shepherd" (Smalcald Articles XII 2).

We should stop for a moment and underscore the absolutely inseparable connection between the doctrine of the church and the doctrine of justification by grace for Christ's sake, through faith. What makes a person a member of the church? This and nothing else, namely, that by the Holy Spirit's work we trust that our sins have been forgiven freely. Such forgiveness comes from God's mercy through Jesus' personal sacrifice on Calvary and His resurrection victory on Easter morning. This is also a useful place to observe that any person who has this confidence is a member of the holy Christian church regardless of the denomination to which he or she might belong. We will have more to say about this later.

When we say that faith joins us to Jesus Christ, we introduce a favorite New Testament designation for the church, namely, the people of God as the "body of Christ." This term, used repeatedly by the apostle Paul, describes the activity of the church as a whole and the part that each individual plays in it.

As the body of Christ, the church is composed of people who are attached to Jesus Christ as their head. (See Ephesians 1:22–23.) Christ rules His members in the sense that they take their direction from Him as their Lord. In addition, the headship of Christ and our allegiance to Him is for the purpose of mutual spiritual care and love for one another. (See 1 Corinthians 12; Ephesians 4:1–16; Colossians 3:10–15.)

Characteristics of the Church

How does one recognize the church, or the body of Christ? To state the matter as simply as possible, the means or instrument that God employs to gather and to preserve the church is the Gospel in all its forms (i.e., the Word and the Sacraments), because only the Gospel can create and sustain saving faith.

Taking the point one step further, because the Holy Spirit works in and through this Gospel to produce faith and in this way to bring people into the church, Lutheran theology teaches that we can recognize the presence of the church wherever the Gospel is proclaimed and wherever the Sacraments are properly administered. So, Word and Sacraments, or the means of grace, are the outward marks or signs of the church.

"It is also taught among us that one holy Christian church will be and remain forever. This is the assembly of all believers among whom the Gospel is preached in its purity and the holy sacraments are administered according to the Gospel" (Augsburg Confession VII 1).

Our definition and discussion of the church will be clearer when we look at some of its basic characteristics, for we confess faith in one holy, catholic, and apostolic church.

At the outset, when we affirm the oneness or unity of the church, we are reasserting what St. Paul said in Ephesians 4:4–6: "There is one body and one Spirit—just as you were called to one hope when you were called—one Lord, one faith, one baptism; one God and Father of all, who is over all and through all and in all." The basic unity of the church is given with the gift; it is not attained by our own efforts but is bestowed by Christ Himself.

What about the many denominations with which we are familiar? The presence of various denominations indicates that there are real and serious differences among Christians concerning important biblical doctrines. Yet this does not mean that the Christian church itself has been cut into many different pieces. Every person in whom the Holy Spirit has worked faith in Jesus Christ—everyone who sincerely confesses Jesus as Lord (1 Corinthians 12:3)—is part of the communion of saints. At this eternally important level, one's sex, social or economic standing, age, race, and denominational membership are not decisive factors. The universal Christian church is inclusive and knows no boundaries.

You are all sons of God through faith in Christ
Jesus, for all of you who were baptized into Christ
have clothed yourselves with Christ. There is neither

Jew nor Greek, slave nor free, male nor female, for
you are all one in Christ Jesus. If you belong to
Christ, then you are Abraham's seed, and heirs
according to the promise. (Galatians 3:26–29)

Are denominations important? Yes, in the crucial sense that they
reflect our unshakable commitment to remain faithful to God's written
Word in Holy Scripture. We have repeated directives from Jesus Himself
that His people are to proclaim and define its divinely revealed message
in its entirety (John 8:31–32; Matthew 28:19–20).

In the interest of revealed truth—and especially in the interest of
retaining the precious Gospel in all of its comfort and power—we evaluate other denominations' public doctrine in terms of faithfulness to Holy
Scripture. But in terms of the oneness of the church, we do not specu-
late with respect to the presence or absence of faith in a person's heart.
God has reserved that right for Himself.

A second important characteristic of the church is its holiness. As we
have observed repeatedly, this is not something Christians have earned
or gained for themselves. We are righteous and holy in God's sight only
because we have been given Christ's righteousness and holiness. He
bestows holiness upon us through faith in the Gospel. Writing to the
ancient church of Corinth, a group that had dubious claims to personal
holiness, St. Paul could nevertheless affirm: "But you were washed, you
were sanctified, you were justified in the name of the Lord Jesus Christ
and by the Spirit of our God" (1 Corinthians 6:11). In short, the church
and the people who comprise it are holy only by virtue of God's act of
justification, by which He declares us righteous. They, in turn, serve God
with holy works.

In addition, the one church is catholic, not in a denominational
way, but in a universal sense. To avoid possible confusion, the Creed in
The Lutheran Hymnal or *Lutheran Worship* uses "Christian" instead of

"catholic." The church is not restricted to any geographical locality or to any group of people. Rather, believers of all races, conditions, and periods of history are part of the church of Christ.

The church is also apostolic. While the original apostles died and cannot be replaced, the church of today stands in continuity with the proclamation and teaching of the first leaders of the church. No one ever has the right to introduce anything in the church other than what is taught in the Word of God, for the church is "built on the foundation of the apostles and prophets, with Christ Jesus Himself as the chief cornerstone" (Ephesians 2:20).

A final characteristic of the church is its invisibility, or hiddenness. This has perhaps been the most misunderstood of all the characteristics. What it means is that one cannot determine by outward appearances who are believers and who are not. Such determination is left to God alone. We do not mean that there are somehow two different churches, one invisible and a separate visible church. Nor do we mean that there are two sides to the church, as though on the one hand there is a visible side and on the other hand an invisible side.

Other Christians

We must distinguish between the church according to its essence— the assembly of true believers in Jesus Christ—and the church according to its outward appearances. In this latter "applied" sense the church includes all those who gather around Word and Sacraments. In the strict sense, this second group can be called "church" only because within it there are true believers in Christ who really do make up the church. In any case, the term "invisible" in relation to the church means only that God— and God alone—can see, know, and identify those who are truly His.

There are many different visible "denominations" within the one holy, catholic, and apostolic church. A denomination represents a number of local congregations sharing the same confession of faith that unite to form a single legal and administrative body. As noted, these congregations ideally have the same doctrinal commitment. In the Lutheran church this commitment is to the inspired Holy Scriptures as the exclusive source and judge of all doctrine and practice, and to The Book of Concord, the confessional writings of the Evangelical Lutheran Church, as an altogether accurate summary and explanation of the content of the Bible.

Congregations have historically joined with other like-minded groups of Christians to form larger organizations in the interest of more effective promotion of the church's God-given mission, as well as for the experience of wider Christian fellowship. Many of the church's responsibilities (e.g., training pastors and teachers, missions, publications, etc.) cannot be carried out adequately by isolated individual congregations. These responsibilities require the cooperative efforts of Christian groups in various locations working together and pooling their material and spiritual resources.

How does a Lutheran Christian interact with believers of other denominations? First, we give thanks to God for any and all groups that honor the triune God and direct people to Jesus Christ as the Son of God and the Savior from sin. As long as this Gospel core is present, these denominations are truly Christian churches.

At the same time, our genuine love for all the people for whom Jesus gave His life does not permit us to overlook departures from biblical truth. The point is that while love is long-suffering and patient, it is also intolerant of error. Doctrinal error is not only a denial of God's revealed truth, but it also jeopardizes a brother or sister's faith. It is important to recall that Christian love prompts Christians to be genuinely concerned about the spiritual well-being of every brother or sister.

Meanwhile, we are exhorted by Jesus Himself to build upon the spiritual unity we already have with every Christian so as to achieve complete concord, or harmony, with the church. In Lutheran theology, this pertains to agreement "in doctrine and in all its articles" (Formula of Concord SD X 31) and in the practical application of this doctrine in the life of the church. This concord is so important that Jesus links its attainment with the mission of the disciples and with those who would believe in Him in the future.

> My prayer is not for them alone. I pray also for
> those who will believe in Me through their message,
> that all of them may be one, Father, just as You are
> in Me and I am in You. May they also be in Us so
> that the world may believe that You have sent Me. I
> have given them the glory that You gave Me, that
> they may be one as We are one: I in them and you
> in Me. May they be brought to complete unity to let
> the world know that You sent Me and have loved
> them even as You have loved Me. (John 17:20–23)

We are thus left with three important and interrelated principles—truth, unity, and love—to which we must be faithful. In practice, this is far easier said than done, and we do not pretend to have the answer to every last question. When by God's guidance two groups have reached agreement in their confession of faith, "pulpit and altar fellowship" can be established between the church bodies (at least no theological reason remains for not declaring such fellowship). This means that at a basic level of worship, members of one group can commune at the other group's altar and pastors can preach in the other group's pulpits.

In the absence of such doctrinal agreement, we might nevertheless cooperate with other groups in more "external" (i.e., nonworship) matters. Sometimes this distinction is difficult to make, but the crucial test question is whether our cooperation in any way clouds, compromises, or renders uncertain our doctrinal confession. In short, do such actions advance the Gospel and are they faithful to it? Note here that the "truth principle" always remains central.

We have seen in these paragraphs that questions of denominational interrelationships can be confusing the first time we confront them. There is no possible confusion, however, when it comes to the function or evangelical task of the church.

Here Jesus' words are explicit: "You will receive power when the Holy Spirit comes on you; and you will be My witnesses in Jerusalem, and in all Judea and Samaria, and to the ends of the earth" (Acts 1:8). In Matthew 28:19–20 we have the Great Commission. The apostles are told to "go and make disciples of all nations, baptizing them in the name of the Father and of the Son and of the Holy Spirit, and teaching them to obey everything I have commanded you. And surely I am with you always, to the very end of the age."

Since the Gospel has come down to us in the form of the written and spoken Word, and also in the visible form of the Sacraments of Holy Baptism and the Lord's Supper, the church's function today consists of administering these means of grace.

Summary

The function of the Christian church is to witness to Jesus Christ. This witnessing activity consists of the faithful use and administration of the means of grace. In all of the church's work, its proclamation of the Gospel must be clear and explicit. This proclamation means witnessing to the unbeliever and encouraging, assuring, and motivating the believer as they live to serve the Lord. Any and all enterprises of the church will either be part of this activity or clearly subordinate to it.

Jesus proclaimed this Gospel while He was active in Palestine for about three years. The apostles carried on His work for much of the first century. Today, as an extension of the preaching activity of Christ and the first apostles, God has given the church a threefold job: (1) faithfully to preach and teach the Word of God; (2) conscientiously administer Baptism and the Lord's Supper; and (3) announce forgiveness to repentant sinners. This responsibility has been given to all believers, and therefore also to each Christian congregation. This is sometimes referred to as the "royal priesthood" or the "universal priesthood," following the lead of such New Testament texts as 1 Peter 2:9 and Revelation 1:6.

To carry out these functions publicly, God has established the public ministry, or pastoral office. This is not merely an extension of the universal priesthood; rather, it is a divine institution in its own right. (See 2 Corinthians 3:6; Ephesians 4:11–12; 1 Timothy 3:1–13; Titus 1:5–9.) God has instructed that pastors—in His name and in the name of the congregations that called them—publicly perform the threefold function of the church outlined above. These pastors are to be respected and honored in spiritual matters, not because they are holier or more pious than other people, but because of their office and their faithfulness to the Word of God. These men are ambassadors, or representatives, of Jesus Christ, whom the Holy Spirit has given to the congregation for its blessing and upbuilding.

The focus of these pages has been on the church as the vehicle through which God brings His message of reconciliation to the world. The whole point is that God wants His Gospel message communicated, and He gears everything in the church to the accomplishment of this objective. And He doesn't leave us to fend for ourselves. When we discuss the function of the church in terms of its proclamation of the Gospel of Jesus Christ, we see that He promises always to be with us (Matthew 28:19–20), and He promises His own Holy Spirit to energize and inform our witness (Acts 1:8).

The Gospel does not conclude with the resurrection or with Jesus' ascension. In a very real sense, the Christian church is part of the Gospel as well. We rejoice in the forgiveness God has given to us freely, with no strings attached. We rejoice, too, that God entrusts to us the responsibility of announcing this forgiveness to people near and far, young and old, of every race and station of life. When we pursue this mission, protected by Jesus' presence and empowered by His Spirit, we participate in the drama of redemptive history.

Discussion Questions

What would you say to a person who said he was a Christian but refused to attend or have anything to do with an organized church?

How would you answer the question "Why are there so many different denominations?"

Do the different church bodies serve a valid purpose?

What is the basic function of the Christian church?

What characteristics or traits would you hope to find in a Christian congregation?

How does your own church meet your expectations?

Discuss the characteristics of the church. What do these mean to a teenager?

11

The End Times

BY PAUL RAABE

Recent books and movies have fueled a great deal of curiosity about what the future will be like. Some people are optimistic, feeling things continually get better. Greater numbers of diseases have cures. Technology accomplishes miraculous things. People are more educated. Some even dream of a utopian, classless society in which everyone works for peace and loves one another.

Others face the future with fear and trembling. They worry that war will destroy the planet. They fear an increase of crime, terrorism, broken families, and lack of basic morality.

Still others are excited because they feel that the end is near. They see the fulfillment of Bible prophecy in the modern political events of the Middle East. They warn that you should fear being "left behind" at the "rapture" lest you suffer in the "tribulation."

What is your attitude about the future? What do the Scriptures teach us about the end times? What does the Bible teach about the end of the world?

Inaugurated Eschatology

The technical word for the end times is "eschatology." Eschatology means the study of the last things. Before we look at what the Scriptures teach about the Last Day, we should first see what they teach about the "last days." We, as Christians, now live in the last days. The end of the ages came with Christ's first coming (1 Corinthians 10:11; Hebrews 9:26; Acts 2:17). The end promised in the Old Testament was inaugurated by Christ's life, death, resurrection, and ascension. Throughout the Old Testament there is a future-oriented thrust. We can summarize its future hope under seven points:

* Old Testament believers waited for a future Redeemer. From Genesis 3:15 on, the Old Testament points toward the promised Suffering Servant (Isaiah 52:13–53:12); messianic King (Isaiah 9:6–7); Prophet (Deuteronomy 18:15); Priest (Psalm 110:4); and glorious Son of Man (Daniel 7:13–14).

* The Old Testament looked forward to the future kingdom of God, when God's rule would be fully experienced by Israel and all the world (Daniel 2:44–45; 7:14, 18, 22, 27).

* The Old Testament promised a new covenant, which would be the fulfillment of God's covenants in the past (Jeremiah 31:31–34).

* The prophets longed for the day when God would restore Israel, His repentant and believing people (Amos 9:11–15; Isaiah 61).

* The Old Testament believers waited for the outpouring of the Spirit on all people (Joel 2:28–29).

* The prophets hoped for the Day of the Lord, when God would defeat His enemies and save His people (Zephaniah 1; 3:9–20; Malachi 4).

* The Old Testament looked forward to a new creation, when the effects of the fall would be reversed (Isaiah 65:17; 66:22; 11:6–9).

With the First Advent (coming) of Christ, these Old Testament hopes were fulfilled. Jesus is the long-awaited Messiah, who ushered in the kingdom of God (Matthew 12:28; Luke 17:20–21; Colossians 1:13). The new Israel (Galatians 3:29; 6:16; Romans 9:6–8) now receives the blessings of the new covenant (1 Corinthians 11:25; Hebrews 8–10). The promised outpouring of the Holy Spirit has already come in Christ (Acts 2; Ephesians 1:13; Titus 3:5–6). And those who are in Christ already participate in the new creation and have eternal life (2 Corinthians 5:17; John 3:16).

When you open the New Testament, you see that this great promised day was inaugurated in Christ. Through the means of grace Christ gives us a share in all of the blessings of this Old Testament hope. The promised end is now, and it is ours by faith.

And yet, Christians still await the fulfillment of these divine promises. They await the second coming of the Redeemer, when the kingdom of God will be fully shown to all (Matthew 8:11–12; 25:34; 2 Timothy 4:18). Christians eagerly anticipate the new covenant, when we will know the Lord perfectly and sin no more (Jeremiah 31:31–34). They long for the day when Christ will gather the entire New Israel, all believers, to be with Him forever (Matthew 24:30–31). The gift of the Holy Spirit, poured out on them in Baptism, is a guarantee that they will be raised with spiritual bodies and inherit eternal life (Romans 8:23; 1 Corinthians 15:44). And they faithfully wait for the Day of the Lord, when they will dwell with Christ forever in the new creation (2 Peter 3:10–13; Revelation 21:1; 1 Thessalonians 5:1–11).

Therefore as a Christian, you live in a tension between the now and the not yet. This tension underlies everything the Scriptures teach about eschatology. On the one hand, the end has arrived in Christ. You have received the promised end-times blessings through the Gospel and Sacraments. You are already a participant in the messianic age.

On the other hand, the end-times blessings you have are yours by faith, not sight (Romans 8:24). The life you have is a life under the cross (Matthew 16:24–27). The fulfillment is still future. Only on the Last Day will you move from a life under the cross to a life of glory.

Future Eschatology

Having seen what Scripture teaches about "inaugurated eschatology" (Christ's First Advent), let's look at what they teach about "future eschatology," the events that belong to Christ's second coming. It is important to keep Christ's First and Second Advents together. The first guarantees the second. The blessings we now receive through the means of grace are the promise of the blessings we will receive on the Last Day.

The Signs of the End

Scripture reveals several signs that herald Christ's return. It may be helpful to organize the signs into three groups.

* *The proclamation of the Gospel to all nations is the most important sign (Matthew 24:14; Mark 13:10). The Great Commission of the church is to "make disciples of all nations" (Matthew 28:18–20), and Christ promises that the gates of hell cannot prevent the church from its mission (Matthew 16:16–10). Yet, we must humbly admit that only God knows when this sign will have been completely fulfilled.*

* *The next group of signs includes disasters: wars, earthquakes, famines, pestilence, and signs in the heavens (Matthew 24:6–8; Mark 13:7–8; Luke 21:9–11, 25–26). These types of disasters have happened throughout history, but the Christian can expect them to intensify toward the end. They give evidence that "the whole creation has been groaning as in the pains of childbirth," awaiting Christ's second coming (Romans 8:18–23).*

* *The third group of signs indicates opposition to God: tribulation, apostasy, and antichrists. Throughout the history of God's people,*

there have been apostasy, tribulation, and many antichrists perse-
cuting God's people. Yet, Scripture teaches that these will intensify
toward the end. There will be an intensified tribulation and perse-
cution against the church (Daniel 12:1; Ezekiel 38–39; Revelation
20:7–9) and an increase of apostasy, or falling away (2 Thessa-
lonians 2:3). The Scriptures also teach that although there are many
antichrists and false Christs (1 John 2:18; 4:3; Matthew 24:24),
there is also one climactic Antichrist (1 John 2:18) or "man of law-
lessness" (2 Thessalonians 2:3–12). He has his seat in the "temple of
God," that is, in the Christian church. He is a pseudo-Christ who
ascribes to himself divine prerogatives, exhibits himself as Christ,
and denies Christ and the truth of the Gospel (2 Thessalonians 2:4,
9; 1 John 2:22; 4:3; 2 John 7). When Christ returns He will slay him
(2 Thessalonians 2:8).

The Lutheran Confessions identify the Antichrist with the office of the pope of Rome. It is important that we note the distinction between the office of the pope and the individual men who fill that office, who may themselves be godly Christians. It is the official claims of the papal office that correspond to the marks of the Antichrist. That office claims to be the "vicar (or substitute representative) of Christ on earth" and claims the right to make infallible doctrine, such as the immaculate conception and assumption of Mary. Martin Luther and his early followers were quite adamant concerning this matter.

Nowhere in Scripture is the establishment of the modern, political state of Israel in 1948 given as a sign of the end. Nor do the Scriptures teach that the "tribulation" takes place after the so-called "rapture" and that it lasts seven years.

Remember this. The purpose of these signs of the end is to assure you of the certainty of Christ's return, not to enable you to set its date (Matthew 24:36; 1 Thessalonians 5:1–3). They have a positive signifi-cance for Christians. When you observe these things happening, you are to "stand up and lift up your heads, because your redemption is drawing near" (Luke 21:28). They serve as a call from God to watchfulness, remaining steadfast in the true faith, holy living, and working for Christ and His kingdom (Matthew 24:42–44; Romans 13:11–14).

The Second Advent of Christ

The Scriptures teach that Christ will return in glory at the end of history at a time known only to God (2 Peter 3:10). He will come visibly, and all people will see Him (Acts 1:11; Matthew 24:30; Luke 17:22–24; 21:27, 35). And He will come in glory, surrounded by the host of His angels (Matthew 16:27). Christians are called to eagerly expect and faithfully await Christ, who will return to save them (Hebrews 9:28).

The General Resurrection

Before discussing the future bodily resurrection, it is important to note what Scripture teaches concerning temporal death and the intermediate state between death and the resurrection.

As a result of the fall, all descendants of Adam are subject to death (Romans 5:12; 1 Corinthians 15:21–22). Since "the wages of sin is death," Christians who are also sinners must pass through temporal death as a judgment upon sin (Romans 6:23). However, for Christians, temporal death is no longer death in the ultimate sense because they are delivered from the divine wrath and eternal death in Christ, who conquered death (1 Corinthians 15:56–57; John 3:16, 18).

Scripture tells little about the intermediate state between temporal death and the resurrection. Popular culture would have one believe that those who die in faith become angels. Others would say that the deceased spend their time in heaven watching over the events of their loved ones here on earth. These and many other ideas about this intermediate state are misguided and wrong.

There are, however, a few clear statements in Scripture concerning this intermediate state. The "spirits" of deceased unbelievers are kept "in prison," a place of punishment (1 Peter 3:19–20). The "spirit," or "soul," of deceased Christians, on the other hand, dwells with Christ in paradise (Philippians 1:21–23; Luke 23:42–43). Nowhere do the Scriptures offer an anthropological or scientific description of this state. Therefore, we should not attempt to explain it on the basis of science or human reason. Rather, we simply affirm what Scripture teaches, that the Christian who dies is with Christ, though apart from his body, an existence that is far better than life in this fallen world.

The physical resurrection of the body remains central to the scriptural teaching of the last things. God's Word clearly teaches that the triune God will raise all the dead at Christ's Second Advent. He will take the believers into heaven, but the unbelievers will receive eternal damnation (John 5:28–29; Acts 24:15; Revelation 20:11–15). The dead shall rise in the same bodies that have died, and they will be glorified—transformed—to be like Christ's glorious body. When Christ returns, the dead in Christ and the Christians who are still living will be "caught up" to meet Him in the air in glory (1 Thessalonians 4:13–17; 1 Corinthians 15:51–57).

Christ's resurrection is the cause and the assurance of our future resurrection (1 Corinthians 15:20; Colossians 1:18; Romans 8:29). Through Baptism, we died and were raised with Christ, which assures our own future bodily resurrection (Colossians 2:12; Romans 6:5, 13). Therefore, we "encourage each other with these words" (1 Thessalonians 4:18) and sing with Paul, "But thanks be to God! He gives us the victory through our Lord Jesus Christ" (1 Corinthians 15:57).

The Final Judgment

The Scriptures teach one final judgment for all people. It will take place at Christ's second coming at the end of history (Matthew 25:31–32; 2 Peter 3:7). "We must all appear before the judgment seat of Christ, that each one may receive what is due him for the things done while in the body, whether good or bad" (2 Corinthians 5:10; see also Romans 14:10–12).

The basis of the judgment is one's relation with Christ. Those who believe in Christ, who are clothed in robes of His righteousness, will be saved. Unbelievers, who rely on their own righteousness, will be damned. The good works of the "sheep" are evidence of saving faith, and the evil works of the "goats" are evidence of unbelief (Matthew 25:31–46). The scriptural teaching of Judgment Day has a very practical significance for our Christian life. It is, first of all, a Law message that warns us and all sinners against carnal security. It calls us to repentance lest we rely on our own righteousness and be condemned. Christ and His righteousness is a Gospel message. We will face Christ, who died and rose for us and comes to save us (Hebrews 9:28). This teaching also encourages us to share the Gospel with our friends and others, so that they, too, will face Christ the Savior and not Christ the condemning Judge.

The New Creation

The Bible teaches that when Christ returns, "new heavens and a new earth" will be created (Isaiah 65:17; 66:22; Revelation 21:1). There is a continuity and a discontinuity between the present world and this new world. On the one hand, Scripture does not portray this future world as an ethereal, "never-never land" off in space somewhere. Rather the new world is portrayed in some sense in continuity with the present creation. For example, as a result of the fall, the ground was cursed (Genesis 3:17–18). Romans 8:19–23 speaks of creation as waiting with eager longing and groaning in childbirth for the time when it will be set free from its bondage to decay. It, too, will become a new creation.

On the other hand, Scripture also teaches that the new creation will be in discontinuity with the world as we know it. The present arrangement of things will pass away; a new heaven and earth will be created and will last forever (Matthew 24:35; 2 Peter 3:10–13; Revelation 21:1). It will be perfect and wonderful.

The new creation will be far more glorious than human language can express. "Now we see but a poor reflection as in a mirror; then we shall see face to face. Now I know in part; then I shall know fully, even as I am fully known" (1 Corinthians 13:12).

Eternal Damnation

Scripture teaches that unbelievers will be condemned to suffer eternal damnation in hell. This is a torment they will suffer consciously in "body and soul" (Matthew 5:29–30; 10:28; 13:41–42; 18:8–9; 25:30) and will endure eternally, without end (Matthew 18:8; 25:46; Revelation 14:11). This torment consists of being excluded from communion with God and experiencing the full force of God's wrath. Unbelievers are already in this state of damnation, which will be fully manifested at Christ's second coming. The cause of man's eternal damnation is found in his unbelief in Christ (John 3:18, 36).

This scriptural teaching is hard for natural man to swallow. People don't like to think about it. Some people are tempted to deny it or weaken its force by substituting other ideas on the basis of human reason. Catholics, for example, teach of purgatory after death. Universalists say that all are somehow saved. Some say the wicked face annihilation rather than eternal suffering.

But the force of this teaching cannot be weakened or denied. It is the strongest form of the Law possible. As with all Law, it leads sinners to recognize their sin and warn them against unbelief and carnal security. The Gospel leads sinners to repentance and salvation.

Eternal Life

Scripture also teaches that those who believe in Christ in "body and soul" will behold God as He is in everlasting joy. The essence of eternal life is presence with God forever—to behold Him as He is (1 John 3:2). The believer already has eternal life (John 3:36) as he exists in a right relationship with God through faith in Christ. Yet in this life the believer knows God only through His Word and the Sacraments of Baptism and the Lord's Supper.

When Christ returns, we will know and see Him face-to-face (1 John 3:2; Revelation 22:4). This life includes perfect freedom from sin, death, and every evil—an eternity of unending joy with God.

Eternal life is found in God alone. The merits of Christ's life, death, and resurrection alone give salvation (Ephesians 2:8–9). Only those who through faith have received Christ's righteousness receive eternal life (John 3:16–18; Romans 3:21–26).

Practical Significance of This Doctrine

The scriptural teaching of the "last things" has great meaning for our lives as Christians. In the midst of sickness and suffering, in the midst of persecution for Christ's sake, we have hope in Christ. We take comfort in the fact that "if God is for us, who can be against us?" (Romans 8:31).

We eagerly await Christ's second coming, when we will be raised from the dead and taken to be with Him forever.

Through the means of grace Christ gives us His guarantee that on the Last Day we will receive His blessings. In Baptism we are raised with Christ (Colossians 2:12), the pledge that on the Last Day you will rise to eternal life (Romans 6:5–8). Through the Lord's Supper Christ gives us a foretaste of the future messianic banquet, which the church will have with Christ (Matthew 26:29; Revelation 19:7–9). Through the Gospel Christ declares us just and acquits us, assuring us that on the Last Day we are justified and receive acquittal (2 Timothy 4:8). By faith we are already participants in the messianic age, assured that we share in the age to come.

This scriptural teaching motivates us to persevere in the true faith and lead a life worthy of our calling (Romans 13:11–14; 2 Peter 3:11–14). It encourages us to proclaim the Gospel to others so that they too might be saved. Throughout our Christian lives, the scriptural teaching of the "last things" should motivate us to serve others and to hope in Christ.

The Millennium

Some Christians talk about a "millennium," which comes from Latin words that mean "a thousand years." Revelation 20 is used as the Scripture proof. "Millennialism" is the belief that at Christ's second coming He will rule on earth from Jerusalem for a thousand years, after which comes the end.

Usually millennialists teach the following (with some variations for the different forms of millennialism):

* *Christ comes secretly and all Christians are "raptured" to meet Him in the air and live with Him in heaven for seven years.*

Meanwhile, on earth the Jewish people convert to the Christian faith and suffer the "tribulation" for those seven years.

At the end of the seven years, several wars culminate in the "battle of Armageddon" a nuclear war centered in the land of Israel. In the midst of Armageddon, Christ returns in glory with the "raptured saints" and sets up an earthly/political kingdom for a thousand years.

After the "millennium," Satan gathers the unbelievers for one final battle against the Jewish people, and after Christ defeats them, the resurrection and judgment of unbelievers occurs. Then comes heaven and hell.

This teaching clearly contradicts the Scriptures. Christ inaugurated His kingdom at His first coming—which will consummate at His second coming. His kingdom is not an earthly, political one (John 18:36). There is only one second advent at the end of history, not two—one secret and one visible. The whole Jewish nation will not be saved; only those who believe in Christ before His second coming (Romans 9:6–8).

In light of the clear passages of Scripture, Revelation 20 should be understood in the following way. At Christ's First Advent, Satan was bound (John 12:31–32; Luke 10:18). The "thousand years" is a symbol of "completeness," the complete period of time from Christ's first coming to shortly before His second. The "first resurrection" refers to Baptism. Those who were raised with Christ through Baptism rule with Christ already (Romans 5:17). At the end of this period, Satan will intensify his persecution of the church and be allowed to hinder its mission outreach for a short time (Matthew 24:15–31). This is "Armageddon" (Revelation 16:16), not a political nuclear war. In the midst of this persecution, Christ returns in glory, and then comes the general resurrection and judgment.

Millennialism is a very dangerous false teaching. It offers people a second chance after the "rapture" and the false hope of an earthly, political kingdom. It also takes the comfort of Christ's kingdom away from the Christian. It teaches that Christ's kingdom exists totally in the future, whereas the Scriptures teach that those who are in Christ now are already participants in the messianic kingdom.

Many people have spent a lot of time trying to compute when, how, and where Jesus will come a second time. It's really an unnecessary effort. Through His Word God gives His children hope for the future. We know that Christ will come again. As Christians we can be sure He will take us to heaven to live with Him eternally. That's what's important to know. The day, place, and time simply make no difference when Jesus is your Savior.

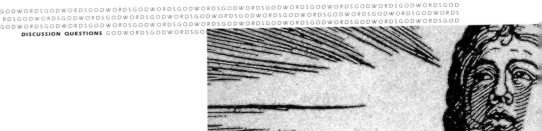

Discussion Questions

Why does the Bible list "signs" that will mark the second coming of Christ?

Do you think it's important or could be helpful if we were able to set a specific date for His coming?

Why do Christians need not fear death?

Why do Christians continue to experience physical death?

Do you think "eternal damnation" is unfair?

What is the purpose of the teaching of "eternal damnation"?

How do you know you are going to heaven?

Is heaven a guaranteed hope for you?

What does our guarantee of eternal life motivate you to do?

A friend tries to convince you about the millennium, the rapture, and Armageddon. He lists names, dates, and places. "You don't believe right," he says. How would you answer this?

12

Does It Really Make a Difference If You Are a Lutheran?

BY TERRY DITTMER

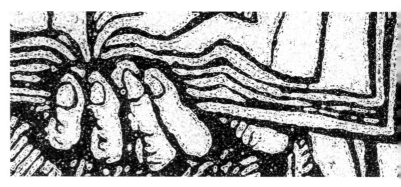

GODWORDSGODWORDSGODWORDSGODWORDSGODWORDSGODWORDSGODWORDSGODWORDSGODWOR
WORDSGODWORDSGODWORDSGODWORDSGODWORDSGODWORDSGODWORDSGODWORDSGODWORDSGODWO
GODWORDSGODWORDSGODWORDSGODWORDSGODWORDSGODWORDSGODWORDSGODWORDSGODWOR

In a day and age when a lot of Christian churches talk about ecumenism and church mergers and looking at how their church is just like any other church, Lutherans, particularly those who are more conservative, tend to look at how they are different.

Add to that a general tendency in our society for people to create a god in their image of god and to make him (or her) into whatever they want god to be. In this twenty-first-century spirituality, anything can be god and all religions, not just Christian denominations, are said to be pretty much the same. In fact, the postmodern trend is to speak of spirituality rather than religion and faith because the latter imply that there are specific things about God and belief that don't change and are all the same. Anyone can be spiritual without needing to be specific about what they "believe." Add to that a general ambivalence about truth. The world says there are no absolutes, but truth is whatever you make it; it's all relative. God changes and truth changes with whatever whim the world seems to blow our way.

Lutherans are a confessional church, which means that we stand on a body of theological documents that explain what Lutherans believe. We Lutherans hold our confessions very dear. We believe they correctly and accurately explain what God's Word teaches. We are very reluctant to compromise our confessional base. We believe it *does* make a difference to believe as Lutherans believe.

First, we believe that THERE IS A GOD, the God of the Bible. It's all about God when it comes to the Christian faith. He is good and generous, faithful and unchanging. He knows all things and is present everywhere. We learn about Him in His Word. He acts or works in all things related to faith.

We are absolutely committed to JESUS CHRIST as Lord and Savior and believe that He died once for all men and women, and through Him alone we are saved. There is no other way to heaven. There is no other way to be saved.

Other religions teach other systems or ways of salvation, but they are doomed to eternal failure because Jesus Christ is not a part of them. Even many Christian groups preach more strongly about social justice and peace on earth. But apart from Jesus Christ, there can be no peace or justice or hope.

Unless a church clearly, boldly, and profoundly preaches and teaches Jesus Christ, it does not live up to its commission to proclaim the love of God. Nor can it truly share the blessings that God would give His people.

We Lutheran Christians have a profound respect for GOD'S WORD. We believe that the Bible is the true, accurate record of God's will for His people. We believe that it makes no mistakes. We believe that the Scriptures tell us all that God wants us to know, especially in matters of salvation.

God's Word is reliable and trustworthy because it is God's Word, not just the product of human thought and imagination.

We proclaim the doctrine of JUSTIFICATION, which means that man is saved solely by the grace of God. Saving human beings is God's work. There is absolutely nothing a person can do to earn salvation or help it on its way. There is no decision that a person can make, no cooperation a person can give. GOD SAVES PEOPLE. He wants all human beings to be saved and guarantees that salvation through Jesus Christ. Salvation is solely God's work.

When someone asks if you have made a decision for the Lord or if you have found Christ, a Lutheran answers, "God has saved me. God found me. I have no doubt that I am saved. It's all about God!"

Lutherans understand BAPTISM as God's faith-giving action in people by the power of the Holy Spirit. It is a Sacrament, not just a rite or ceremony. It is not something you do. It is God's seal on His people. It is God saying through water and His Word that the baptized person belongs to Him. To that end, we baptize children. The child does not need to make a decision to be baptized because Baptism is God working faith in the child. Again, it's all about God!

SANCTIFICATION is another Lutheran hallmark. We believe God's Spirit is active and working in the lives of believers, helping us to live as God's people. We realize living a Christian life can be a challenge and a struggle, but we know God daily and richly guides and blesses us and forgives us when we fail. While we strive to live a God-pleasing life, we do not suggest that the sanctified life leads to helping along our salvation. Living a Christian life is a Spirit-inspired, joyful response to God's love for us in Christ.

The LORD'S SUPPER is the second Sacrament through which the Christian receives assurance of the forgiveness of sins and the promises of faith. God nourishes His people as He reminds them of His love for them. In bread and wine we receive Christ's body and blood, through which we are renewed and refreshed. The Lord's Supper is not just a ceremony or a magic act in which bread and wine are changed into body and blood. It is God's gracious way of renewing His people. Lutherans believe they should participate in the Lord's Supper often.

Lutherans understand God's FORGIVENESS to be generous, unmerited, and without condition. We don't work to earn forgiveness because we'd never make it. Rather, when we confess our sins, we know God, in love and mercy, forgives and puts those sins behind us. The record is erased, and He never looks back. This, in turn, moves us to live life confidently and hopefully.

Many church people say you have to "feel" your faith and look for emotional, spiritual highs. Lutherans are careful to understand that emotions are tricky and that, as human beings, we are subject to highs and lows—sometimes we're on a roller coaster of feelings. If we are always looking for religious highs or mountaintops, we may easily be disappointed.

Consequently, Lutherans stress the need for knowledge and understanding of God's Word and what it has to say to God's people. We stress that we ought not rely on our emotions as a barometer of faith. We give thanks to God that even in down times, when we are not feeling particularly close to God, we can still know that we are saved, despite our failing emotions. Our faith is not dependent on the way we feel!

Lutherans don't spend a lot of time trying to figure out when Jesus is going to return or exactly how it will happen. We believe that Jesus will return! We believe that He will come to judge. We believe that He will welcome all believers into heaven.

There are a lot of Christians who talk about the millennium, the rapture, Armageddon, and other eschatological (big word for "the end times") jargon. But trying to figure out the date and time is a waste of time. The Bible tells us that Christ will come as a thief in the night. No one knows the day or hour except the heavenly Father. It serves absolutely no purpose to worry about when He's coming. We need only know that He *is* coming. To that end, we want to make sure we are ready, and by the power of the Holy Spirit guiding and directing our lives, we *will* be.

Lutherans have been traditionally and historically careful about those with whom they are in FELLOWSHIP, meaning with whom they share the Lord's Supper and who may preach from their pulpits. This is not because we believe we are better than anybody else. It is not because we believe that only Lutherans are going to heaven. Rather, it is to present before the world a clear testimony to what we believe. Our understanding of the doctrines of justification and sanctification and the Sacraments of the Lord's Supper and Baptism could be compromised if we are not careful.

If, for example, I receive the Lord's Supper as a Lutheran, understanding that in the Sacrament God nourishes me personally, touches me personally with His love, while the person next to me, from a Reformed-church background, believes that Communion is just a ceremony to demonstrate unity, are we not doing and believing two different things? What unity is there in that? Both persons' beliefs are compromised, and a clear witness is given to no one.

Another concern is prayer, not so much with other Christians, but with other religious people. Should a Christian pray in the company of non-Christians? The concern is that if a Christian prays in the company of a Muslim, Buddhist, Hindu, New Age practitioner, or other religious person, he or she may give the impression that there are many gods and they are all equal. That impression compromises the faith we have in the true God of the Bible and is a witness we want to avoid. We don't want to compromise our faith under any circumstance.

Lutherans believe we have a responsibility to share the GOSPEL, namely God's Good News of salvation through Jesus Christ, and to clearly WITNESS to others what we believe. It is our privilege to share with others what we know about God's love, what we know about God's truth, and how we can trust and hope in Christ. We want people to know how God works in people, how He will bless their lives on earth, and how He will bring them into heaven for all eternity. We don't like to be quiet about what we know for sure. The world is offering all kinds of alternative spiritualities. We want the whole world to know God's truth.

It does make a difference whether a person is a Lutheran, a Baptist, a Roman Catholic, a Methodist, a Presbyterian, or whatever. It is not that Lutherans think themselves superior to anyone else. Rather, we want to make a bold and clear confession of our faith in Jesus Christ and our understanding of how God works in the lives of His people. It's all about God!

Discussion Questions

Mormons are often described as good, God-fearing, outstanding moral people. Tenets of their faith include the following: they accept Joseph Smith's Book of Mormon as divinely inspired; they do not accept the divine nature of Jesus; they say all men will become gods and insist on a strict, moral lifestyle. Based on your reading, how should Lutherans respond to Mormons?

A Baptist friend says you should be rebaptized since you were baptized as an infant. She says you need to make a decision for the Lord and choose to follow Him. What would you say to her?

A friend has a low opinion of himself. He hates who he is and thinks life has dealt him a worthless hand. He feels like junk and has even talked about suicide. What hope do you have to offer?

A Christian friend invites you to her church and you decide to go. You discover that the Lord's Supper is to be celebrated. Your friend wants you to go to the altar with her. "We're all Christians," she says. You know her church has a different understanding of Communion than you do. What are you going to do?

Discussion Questions

A friend tells you he leads a good life, tries to do what's right, and thinks God will take him to heaven. After all, if God is loving and merciful, He won't send nice people to hell. What would you say to him?

Even though we've studied and learned about our faith, it can be difficult to talk to our friends. Why is what we believe so hard to talk about? What could God give you to make you a better witness?

Does it make a difference to you that you are a Lutheran? Why or why not?

Do you think you'll always be a Lutheran? What if you marry someone who is a member of another church? How would you decide what church to attend? What problems are there in spouses trying to be members of their own church?

What is important to you when you join a church? Sermons? Worship services? Youth activities? Music? Theology? Fellowship and other activities?